SIX SQUARE METERS

Margaret Simons is an award-winning freelance journalist and author, and a journalism academic at the University of Melbourne. She has published thirteen books, including biographies of the Australian Minister for Foreign Affairs, Penny Wong, and *Malcolm Fraser: the political memoirs*, which won book of the year and best nonfiction book at the 2010 NSW Premier's Literary Awards. In the past, Simons has worked for *The Age* and *The Australian* newspapers. As a freelancer, she has had work published in dozens of magazines and newspapers in Australia and overseas.

TO THE FAMILY SHRUBBERY

Scribe Publications
18–20 Edward St, Brunswick, Victoria, Australia 3056
2 John St, Clerkenwell, London, WC1N 2ES, United Kingdom
3754 Pleasant Ave, Suite 223w, Minneapolis, Minnesota 55409 USA

First published by Scribe 2015
This edition published 2026

Book design by Allison Colpoys
Typeset in Adobe Garamond 11/16.5 pt

Printed and bound in the UK by CPI Group (UK) Ltd, Croydon CR0 4YY

Scribe Publications is committed to the sustainable use of natural resources and the use of paper products made responsibly from those resources.

978 1 964992 36 5 (US edition)
978 1 925106 83 1 (Australian edition)
978 1 925307 10 8 (ebook)

A catalogue record for this book is available from the National Library of Australia.

scribepublications.com.au
scribepublications.co.uk
scribepublications.com

SIX SQUARE METERS

REFLECTIONS FROM A SMALL GARDEN

Margaret Simons

SCRIBE
Melbourne | London | Minneapolis

INTRODUCTION

They say that you reap what you sow. This is one of those annoying aphorisms that are at once absurdly obvious and very cruel. It can be read to mean that we earn our misfortunes. If you are in the middle of a misfortune, this is not something you want to be told. We all have faults, shameful compulsions, blindspots, and secrets but it is harsh, sometimes, to be told that our lives are of our own making. What about all the things you sow that don't germinate? The aphorism-writer would doubtless say that this was because of your neglect. You did not water sufficiently. You failed to achieve that mantra of the scary gardening books, 'eliminate all perennial weeds'. You failed to achieve 'a fine tilth'. (I challenge anyone to manage to throw the word 'tilth' into casual conversation. It belongs only in intimidating texts on cultivation and in Scrabble games.) The aphorism-writer fails to account for the fact that sometimes seed is dead. The fact that dried up specks of seed grow into plants is, like most miracles, not to be relied upon. Things die, or fail to live.

And what about all the things you didn't sow but that you

end up reaping anyway? Aphorism writers and the authors of depressing gardening books fail to acknowledge bad luck, and the fact that some of the things we sow are those we didn't even realize we had with us — like the dandelion seeds that float in the wind, and the burrs that stick to our socks, and the couch grass that adheres to our boot, until it gracefully relinquishes its hold to take root. A fine tilth for one is a fine tilth for all. In fact, nothing is more guaranteed than a fine tilth to ensure that you will reap not only what you have sown, but opportunistic weeds as well.

Normally, gardening aphorisms and parables are full of earthy truth, but this one should be re-written. Sometimes you reap what you sow. Sometimes you reap what other people sowed. Sometimes you haven't got a clue what you are sowing, and sometimes you just get lucky, or unlucky. All these things are true of life, as of gardening.

The cause of these reflections is beginning this little book on gardening, and trying to think why it is that I continue to garden, even though I am not very good at it. Why does it give me such pleasure and, let me admit, such frustration and misery? The aphorism, and so many other sayings and metaphors, tell me why. Gardening is not only a way of passing the time and growing useful and beautiful things, it gives me the schema for thinking about life. I am now in my 50s. I spend quite a bit of time reflecting on the things that I have sown and the things that I have reaped, and all the accidents along the way.

If you are to read on, then you need to agree to some terms of engagement. I am not an expert, and this is not a how-to book.

At times in the past, when I have written about my garden, I have been approached by the Open Gardens scheme to see if I would be interested in throwing my premises open to the public. I have never done so and will never do so. The idea fills me with horror. My garden is always a mess and a failure as much as a success.

I hate all garden orthodoxies. Well, that is not quite true. I was drawn to permaculture for a while, but it is a bit like visiting Ikea. I like the IDEA of living like that, in a virtuous, well managed, and tidy fashion, but the reality of trying to achieve it is too much, and leaves me feeling inadequate. Permaculture at its worst is guilt inducing, leading one to question the utility of a rose.

So do not read on if you want to know how to garden. Rather, this little book is a record of my gardening-related reflections over the course of the last few years. Some parts have been published before in *Melbourne Review* and *Adelaide Review*, where I had a gardening column for a while. Some parts refer back to earlier parts of my gardening life, but by and large what you will read here is a collection of the things I think about when I am in the garden, or wishing I was in the garden.

I am best known as a journalist. I write on politics and media, and I have written biography. This can make enemies. Over the years, some commentators have suggested that my views on public life and journalism are to be taken less seriously because I have also written about compost, vegetables, and chickens. One is either a serious journalist or a gardening writer, apparently. Not both. Well, bollocks to that. In public I sometimes use the line that what unites my journalism and my gardening is muckraking.

That usually gets a laugh. The truth is more fundamental, and harder to express.

Through the years since I planted my first seed, I have found that the seasonal metaphors, the gardening-related insights, are the ones that make most sense to me. I talk about the first drafts of my books as being like compost heaps — fetid messes that might, nevertheless, eventually mature into useful stuff. I talk to my children, now navigating the transition from childhood to adulthood, about growth and pruning. It has been this way for many years now.

I'd like to say it started in childhood, but that wouldn't be true. My mother was a gardener, but my sister and I regarded her lawn mowing, her trips to the country to collect horse manure, and her spreading of blood and bone with disgust and contempt.

I left home in my early twenties and fetched up in the inner suburbs of Melbourne in a share house that had a tiny backyard with a single garden-bed. It had been used by a previous resident to grow marijuana, and the crop had gone wild. Operation Noah was coming around. Back then, this was an annual police campaign in which people were encouraged to dob in drug growers and dealers. In a fit of paranoia, the housemates ripped out the marijuana remnants, leaving bare earth.

The house had an outside toilet, which meant that several times a day I passed that sad, little, bare garden bed. I am not sure what made me do it, but one weekend I bought a packet of runner bean seeds at the supermarket and planted them out. Within days they were above the earth, their little leaves unfurling from the spear shapes that had pierced the soil's crust. Weeks later, we were harvesting handful after handful of crisp green pods, and I was hooked.

I was profoundly ignorant about gardening, and I read books to fill in the gaps. My first gardening book, which I still own, was written by two grim-faced men who were pictured in towelling hats and tight shorts, dispensing advice on chicken manure and brassicas. They brooked no departure from their methodology. There was a right way and a wrong way. The right way was fine tilth and clipped edges. I still love that book, but I haven't used it for years. It takes time, when you have learned from books, to forgive yourself for having onions that are not in straight lines and seedbeds that are not cultivated to that fine tilth.

In this context, the permaculture books were particularly thrilling with their lovely line drawings, and visions of an interlocked universe. When I moved to another share house, with a bigger garden, I spent many hours fussing around with keyhole beds and vast quantities of expensive lucerne hay. But gardening books are to gardening what childcare books are to babies, pornography to sex, *Home Beautiful* magazine to housing, and a literal reading of the Bible to Christianity. Counsels of perfection don't work for me. I am too messy. I am not a fundamentalist. My edges are not clipped; my tomatoes sprawl unpruned and unstaked.

Fifteen years ago, when my children were little, I was living far from any beaten track in the Blue Mountains of New South Wales. I kept goats that were named after my daughter's kinder friends, a rooster called Vronsky, and a crowd of chickens. It was a time of almost self-sufficiency. It was not idyllic. There were tough times, and great sadness as well as the joy of watching my babies grow. It was *intense*. What kept me sane was watching the chickens, and fooling around with my giant vegetable patch. I had no fewer than three compost heaps — proof of humble resurrection, and the triumph of life over death.

That season of life came to an end, and the children and I moved to the inner city, where I now live in a semi-detached house in sight of the city towers, but with hardly any space for gardening.

The inner city suits me, and my teenagers, but a couple of years ago, as life once again grew particularly intense, I found myself thinking that when I retired I would return to gardening.

Then I thought, 'Why wait?'

There were a few reasons, the first one being lack of space. At the front, my house faces a post office staffed by heroic women who deal with all the joys and stresses of the suburb: speaking to people of all nations as they navigate the paying of bills, the making of deposits and passport applications, and that basic act of citizenry, joining the electoral roll. Facing the post office, I have about two-and-a-half square meters of soil in a narrow strip between my house and the fence.

At the back I have a brick-paved space, six meters square, with two raised garden beds, one of which is entirely in shade. This backyard opens on to a bluestone-paved laneway, and on the other side is the carpark of a McDonald's restaurant.

Nevertheless, I started to garden, and it made my life better. Now, each morning before I rouse the children from bed and walk the ancient Labrador, I engage in a ritual I laughingly refer to as 'walking the grounds'. I pick anything that has ripened. I climb a stepladder to view the four polystyrene boxes on the roof, which are filled with seasonal vegetables and herbs. I contemplate the pots on the verandah, and observe the fall of shadow in the back lane between my house and McDonald's, and consider what will grow there. Inner suburbs being what they are, I also check whether the rat bait has been taken.

Lots of things don't work. I have become expert in what will grow with next to no sunlight. I grow mostly vegetables and herbs, but also some nutritionally challenged ornamentals. There is a lemon tree, and a bay tree, and a mandarin tree under threat of replacement because it doesn't fruit. Sometimes life gets busy, and it all goes to weeds. There is failure as well as success, rat bait as well as fresh lettuce, things that die as well as those that live. It is ridiculous, because life is ridiculous, and because gardening in such a tiny space most certainly seems that way.

Yet 'walking the grounds' each morning makes me unreasonably happy, and, being who I am, I find myself writing about it, either at the keyboard or in my head. This book is the result of that.

I am grateful for the chance to share it.

SUMMER

My vegetable garden is presently a source of pride and shame. So many things are fruiting and making themselves available for harvest that I could feel like a real gardener if I focused on this alone.

On the other hand, the weeds are obscuring the tops of the carrots. The parsnips have gone to seed and their great spindly brown tops dominate everything, and the tomatoes have blossom end rot — an unsightly and wasteful disease encouraged, I believe, by inconsistent watering; too much flood and drought, and not enough drip irrigation, a problem I must fix.

In particular, my zucchini are both a joy and an embarrassment. I planted three zucchini seeds back in October, expecting only a couple to survive my neglect and the attentions of the snails. All grew to adulthood against the odds and now, at peak harvest time, when pumpkins are being brought in to be stored, when onion tops are turning brown and apples are turning red, and when herbs are putting on their last rush of growth, the zucchini are fruiting in profusion.

Every vegetable gardener knows that if you leave a small zucchini on the plant for a couple of days, it will be a marrow. If you are mounting a harvest festival display, big zucchini look very impressive, but for eating, they are hopeless. There are recipes for stuffed marrow, but in my opinion life is too short to stuff any vegetable. Therefore, zucchini must be picked quickly once formed. They do not freeze well, and must be eaten within days.

It is true that freshly picked zucchini have a juiciness and flavor unmatched by the shop-bought product, but all the same I have had enough of them. And enough zucchini cake too. And enough ratatouille, zucchini fritters, and char-grilled zucchini dip.

Today, despite my best efforts at regular and thorough harvesting, I discovered one of those zucchini marrows hidden under the leaves. It was huge. I could hardly lift it. Goodness knows how many baby zucchini could have been borne by this plant had it not been devoting its energies to this whopper. All that water and all those nutrients, locked up and pumping their way around this overgrown phallic symbol.

I dragged the marrow out of the narrow strip of land at the front of my house, and down the passageway to the kitchen. I cut it open. Inside, it was beautiful. The flesh was creamy, instead of pale-green or white. The seeds, which are little more than a channel of wetness in the smaller fruit, were fully formed, white and slithery. The whole enormous fruit was bursting with life and the urgency of reproduction. In just a few seconds, the cut edges of the zucchini were studded with little dewdrops of sap, so fast was moisture being pumped through the flesh.

I thought briefly, and in a depressed sort of way, about stuffed marrow, but I knew I couldn't be bothered. I sliced the zucchini in half again, and again, and again, and fed it to the compost heap.

~

There must be a direct neurological connection between the receptors in our noses and our emotions. Nostalgia, joy, revulsion, and depression can all enter through the nostrils, proving that we are still creatures of sense as much as sensibility. This is one of the reasons the garden, or rather my backyard, is such a rich place to be. In a few moments, I travel from the revolting smell of the bag of blood and bone by the back fence (must put it away) through the ambivalence of the compost heap (sweetness and decay in equal measure), to the bliss of brushing against the tomato and basil plants growing in pots on the verandah. And, living where I do, all this is accompanied by the smell of McDonald's. They have some very fancy extractor machinery that in theory prevents the burger odor from bothering the neighbors, but on a hot day with a strong wind it is only partly effective.

We have the windows open at this time of year, as well. Normally, the double-glazing protects us from the sounds of the drive-through, but with the house open to the city air our every movement seems punctuated by the ubiquitous question asked of drivers over the too-loud PA system. 'Would you like fries with that?' The song of the fries, which are always proffered and rarely refused, accompanies my evening watering. It becomes quite musical, if you allow yourself to think that way.

At this time of year, each evening finds me in the backyard, mosquitoes at heel, watering the garden. It is a ritual that accompanies the cessation of the day's heat. The silverbeet recovers from the wilting temperatures in an astonishing fashion. One moment it seems dead, flopping on to the soil. A little water flowing in to those veins, and in minutes it stands — proud, glossy, and green. I revive it in order to kill it. A quick slash with the knife, and we have leaves for dinner. The end of the day's heat is also the time for harvest.

Watering the garden is almost meditative. My back to the house, my mind at rest, I try to judge how much water is enough, and not too much, for plants that have stood all day in the parching sun. This involves an interaction with the minutiae of my tiny patches of soil. Gardeners know their gardens with the intimacy of a lover. Just as lovers know each dip and rise of flesh, so a gardener knows the contours of the soil. The jet of water from my hose kicks up dirt. Even though the soil is dry, it takes some time for it to accept water. The earth is like a sponge left to dry for too long. It has forgotten how to drink. I can judge how long to let the hose play on each spot, where there is a small dip in which water will pool and thus be absorbed, and where the soil is so sloped that water runs off long before reaching the roots of the plants.

Lakes form, then overflow, then tip their contents into neighboring hollows. I know how long this will take, and the order in which the little holes will fill. I can judge it almost to the moment, and I shift the hose just before the deluge. Then there is a pause while the water sits on the dry earth. Am I imagining the tension? Suddenly, as though a mouth has been opened, the water disappears. Then I can return with the hose, and the garden drinks deep.

With my pot plants, though, water runs out of the bottom long before the soil is soaked. A slow drip feed is what's needed, but who has the time for that? Inside the house there are jobs to do. Washing to be put on. Dishes to clear. Work clothes to prepare. So I create my little floods and then move on. Always, I resolve that before summer comes again, I will create a drip irrigation scheme as a counter to my busyness and my impatience.

One of the difficulties of gardening in a small space is finding a way of doing the job without wrecking everything else that is going on. If I overwater the lemon tree, the water runs out of the pot, across the brick paving, and disrupts my step-grandson's Lego town — although he seems quite pleased with the idea of a flood to enliven the evenings of his plastic, square-headed population.

When I water the lettuce, strawberries, beans, and tomatoes on the sundeck, I have to first make sure that the washing line underneath is empty or everyone will be wearing clothes with earth-colored streaks.

Tonight I am soaking the seeds of moonflowers, ready for planting out tomorrow. Moonflowers grow on long vines. They can put on five meters in a single year. I have read that the flowers open in the early evening and close before noon the following day. You can actually watch them open, it happens so fast. Their fragrance is sweet and heavy. I plan to plant them in the gap between the brick pavers at the foot of the steps that go from verandah to backyard. My hope is that they will climb up the balustrade and that next summer, the moonflowers and their fragrance will accompany me during the evening watering and harvest ritual.

~

I walked out into my backyard this morning in order to recover from some news. I had heard that a friend of mine had died. I had known she was ill. I had intended to visit. I left it too late.

She had one of those cruel wasting diseases that leave the mind intact while the body gradually ceases to work. She knew she was dying. Her husband Peter told me that in the last few days there was a sense of peace, and of permission having been given for her to leave this life. Her children were grown and well. Her husband was resigned to losing her. Peter recalled his mother's death. Apparently, her last words were 'I never knew it could be so wonderful.' She meant death. Peter's wife didn't say those words, but the feeling, he said, was similar. The leaving of life was as it should be — except too soon. And right away the cynic in me wonders if it could really have been like that, or whether this is just what those of us left behind choose to believe — that death can be wonderful, that there is such a thing as a good death.

The news, and my long conversation with Peter, carried me back to an earlier time in my life. This couple were crucial to me. It was largely through my friendship with them that I first dared to call myself a writer. I had already published one book when I met them, but I was not a writer. I had merely written.

It takes readers to make a writer, and their great talent was reading. Peter and Libby were the best, most instinctive, perceptive, and careful readers I have ever met. They saw your intention, and they saw the things you didn't know you were trying to achieve. They told you what you were doing in such a way that you could see it for yourself. They could fulfil that profound imperative of E.M. Forster's — *only connect.*

> *Only connect the prose and the passion, and both will be exalted, and human love will be seen at its height. Live in fragments no longer.*

It takes great readers to achieve that kind of connection. No writer can do it on their own, or at all. Sometimes I think the talent of reading is rarer than the ability to write, and I wish that more people would devote themselves to great reading, rather than join all of us who for some reason feel a need to add to the world's written words.

And so I walked in the garden to reflect on this loss. It is about three years since I last saw Peter and Libby. While they were frequently in my thoughts, I hadn't rung, I hadn't written. I had made plans to visit, but I left it all too late. And, in the garden, the lettuce has all run to seed, the leaves on the purple king beans have the mottled look that comes with stress, and the passionfruit vine is putting out small, wrinkled fruit. It seems incapable of getting sufficient water to its extremities to combat the effects of forty-degree heat.

Summer is, in the pagan tradition, the time of full fruit. It is the tipping point of the year, when one prepares for harvest and the preservation of bounty. I wish. Instead, my garden is ragged, and the weekends have been so hot that I have not had the will to get out there and repair, replant, and recoup.

Someone once wrote a poem about Libby. I remember it being shared with the small group of writers that, at that time in my life, gathered around the Varuna Writers' Centre in the Blue Mountains. It was an observation of her in the garden, travelling back and forth to the garden beds on a crisp, cold day with her wheelbarrow, her jeans muddy and her cheeks red. It was an observation of her beauty.

And so, too late, I have booked my flights, and will go back to that place and visit my remaining friend, and we will reflect on the past, the present, and the future.

~

It all happened so quickly. It was too hot to garden. I was sitting at the computer trying to write, interrupted continually by children and the telephone. Then my partner came in.

'What?' I said rather crossly.

'There's smoke in the sky. I'm going up to the signal box to see what's happening.'

That was seventeen years ago (at the time of writing in 2015). I had just returned from the maternity hospital, having given birth to my son, my second child. We were living in an old renovator's delight in the Blue Mountains, alongside the railway line. Our home was, in fact, the old stationmasters' house for a disused station on the main Western line out of Sydney. From the signal box on the embankment above us, you had a view of the valleys on either side.

I took the baby out to the sundeck to breastfeed him while our toddler played in the paddling pool. The sky was now half full of smoke. It seemed to have gotten thicker and darker astonishingly quickly, and the sunlight was odd and orange, casting strange shadows and lights on the water of the paddling pool. Later, I learned the fire was at this stage leaping ridges, killing firefighters, travelling with astonishing speed.

My partner came back. 'It's a big fire …' he said. Then the signalman called down to him. 'They're evacuating the coal mine.' The coalmine was only a couple of kilometers away from us.

'Get the children ready to go,' my partner said. It was only about a quarter of an hour since he had seen the first sign of smoke. Moments later, the sky was full. There was no blue to be seen, and I was bundling the baby and the toddler into the car, so frantic I didn't have time to heed the rising tide of fear. No time to pack a nappy bag. No time to get a change of clothes for myself. We were off, down the dirt road with only a moment to say goodbye. This was my first trip away from home since being discharged from hospital.

I looked in the rear vision mirror at the fruit trees I had planted over the last three years, and at the still untamed blackberry clumps, and at the chickens pecking nervously through the mulch, and at the sundeck, completed only a few weeks ago and planned as the focus of our summer. It was hard to believe this was happening. At six o'clock, my partner telephoned me at the friends' house where I had taken refuge. The fire was expected to pass to the north of us, through the coal mine. At seven, he was to phone again. The call never came. The phone lines were down.

'Clarence and the famous Zig Zag railway are ablaze,' the radio told me. These were the nearest identifiable spots to our home. I cried. The emergency information numbers were constantly engaged. For three hours, there was no information, then railway staff at a nearby station told me that our house was still standing, and that my children's father had been seen. This time, tears seemed inadequate.

The children and I came home after spending three nights away due to smoke and continuing hazards from burning embers. The bushfire was still burning, but to the north of us. The bushfire brigades were superb. We had crews from as far away as South Australia parked on our front lawn, ready to protect us. They were well organized, on top of things, full of the deceptive laconic attitude of those who deal with emergency, know what they are doing, and do it well. Can there be any evidence of everyday, persistent human goodness more convincing than a bushfire brigade? I doubt it.

In the weeks that followed, we lived in a small patch of untouched bush surrounded by acres of black trunks and burnt leaves. Our magpie family survived, so too the currawongs, but we feared that our wallabies, which used to come up to the front lawn every evening, were dead. There would have been so much activity — fire trucks, and people in bright yellow uniforms. We thought they must have panicked and fled in the wrong directions.

Then, almost a full week after the fires, three of the six were back, nibbling their way across the grass and sniffing the burnt smells. The joey, which used to gad about from adult to adult like a toddler on springs, was nowhere to be seen. His mother was missing too, but the other adults looked whole, if shattered and more than normally tame. We put out bowls of water for the animals that gradually began to crowd into our little green refuge, desperate for food and moisture. There were snakes, and lizards, and an increasing tribe of wombats, and wallabies, and every bird known to the bush. We were a Noah's Ark in a sea of destruction.

The destruction was random. A waratah by the side of the road on the way into town had survived, red on black. The mountains around us were a snakes-and-ladders board of brown swathes and untouched green. The washing I had hung out on the day of the fire had charred marks from burning embers, but our house was undamaged, and we were fine, and the garden was still growing.

Two weeks after our return I put fresh sheets on our bed, not realizing that one of them had been on the washing line during the bushfires. Our bed smelt of eucalyptus smoke, and in the middle of the night, I woke to find the children's father, who stayed with the house through the worst of the firestorm, tossing and turning and twitching in the grips of a nightmare in which we were all burning, and about to die.

Having lived through those times, can I be blamed for no

longer liking summer? Now I live in the inner city I am unlikely to be personally at risk, but nevertheless the habit I acquired during those years, of scanning the horizon and sniffing the wind, has not left me in the eight years since I moved away from my bushfire-prone home.

Summer used to be a worry-free time, all relaxation and fun. Now we worry all the time. Summer is seriously stressful. After the Black Saturday bushfires in Victoria, the whole state was in mourning. Everyone knew somebody who had lost their home, or their life. We have not yet recovered from that trauma, and the awareness that on any hot, windy day it will be happening again, for someone, somewhere. Nor can we recover from the knowledge that it is going to get worse as our climate changes. The baby I had just given birth to seventeen years ago is now a strapping young man who tells me I worry too much. Yet forevermore, I suspect, every enjoyment associated with summer — from ripe fruit to time at the beach — is tainted by the knowledge and the fear that we could all have died that day.

—

I used to be no fan of Christmas. It doesn't touch my pagan heart. It is always the pagan festivals that make the most sense to me, and the Christian ones pack the most punch when they stick closest to the basic way of life: the birth, death, and resurrection with which all gardeners are familiar, and around which they structure their year.

Christmas, in the traditions that preceded Christianity, was the winter solstice — the turning point of the season, at which time it seemed both fitting and necessary to eat the nuts, and dried fruits, and preserved hams that had been laid down for sustenance through the hard months. One could kill the goose, or the turkey, because the year was about to enter its upswing, and spring would come again.

But we celebrate Christmas at the other end of the cycle, near the summer solstice, and the tipping point of the year before the descent into death. Any good pagan knows that life is a duality. When a cycle is at its peak, the reverse is just around the corner. Fruit ripens, then decays. The full is the empty. Life incorporates death.

In this context, 'Tis the season to be jolly' seems to me a motto guaranteed to depress. Christmas has become the mania of a bipolar society, and the blackness always seems to me to be very near at hand, hiding under the tinsel and glitter, but unacknowledged. New Year is a much better festival, a psychologically healthy time of year, being about review, reflection and fresh resolution, realistic regret and reasonable hope.

~

I have been cruel to the eggplant. I love eggplant but I have never succeeded in getting them to fruit. Now I have three plants growing in polystyrene fruit boxes on the roof. The trick, I know, is to make them think they are going to die. That way they will hurry up and reproduce. So I starved them of water, then gave them just enough to survive. It was a finely judged thing. Too much kindness, and there was no point. Too much cruelty and they would die. During the hot weather last week, I wandered periodically to the roof to observe the degree of wilt.

One of my favorite cookery writers, Geoff Slattery, once said that if Gough Whitlam had been a vegetable, he would have been an eggplant, but that he would have called himself an aubergine. I know what he meant. The kingly purple, the elegant curves of the leaves, their fussy, arrogant ways ... but analogies can only be carried so far. Nobody I know ever made Gough Whitlam wilt.

Nevertheless, I play with the analogy as I wander around the backyard, thinking in that crazy, non-accountable way that gardens inspire. I think of vegetables and politics. John Howard is definitely a brassica. Kim Beazley was a potato. Julia Gillard is, I think, a legume — a nitrogen fixer, but a short-lived annual. Paul Keating was a member of the onion family — elegant and tall, lots of layers. It is a while, I think, since we have had any tomatoes, any basil, any garlic or aubergines, in politics.

It is in Shakespeare's *Richard II* that the gardeners, making their way humbly through the gardens and courtyards of a great palace, wonder why their monarch doesn't take the same care of the kingdom as they do of the garden.

An under-gardener asks his master:

Why should we, in the compass of a pale,
Keep law, and form, and due proportion,
Showing, as in a model, our firm estate,

When our sea-walled garden, the whole land,
Is full of weeds, her fairest flowers chok'd up,
Her fruit trees all unprun'd, her hedges ruin'd,
Her knots disorder'd and her wholesome herbs swarming with caterpillars?

He never really gets an answer, but the gardeners presumably keep on gardening, as in the larger garden, kings are deposed and crowned, murdered and made.

I think I have left all my cruelty to the eggplant far too late, because things are already beginning to feel autumnal. It is the season for cutting things back — trimming the heads on the lavender, so they will grow into bushes instead of going all leggy. 'Cutbacks,' I whisper as I go around with my shears. 'Rationalization.'

I have also been thinking about the winter jobs I will do when everything is dormant and uncharacteristically neat — when my little nation doesn't need my constant management, and I can turn my mind to planning. 'Infrastructure,' I mutter. I am thinking not of roads and railways and communications, but of herb boxes and trellises, garden paths and micro-watering systems.

Meanwhile, my cruelty has been precise and successful. All the eggplants are flowering. Now it is a race against time to see if they fruit before it gets too cold.

—

It rained last night. The deluge arrived in a great rush of thunder and lightning. We had a power cut right in the middle of watching *Game of Thrones*, and I was plunged from that gaudy, ghastly imaginary world to the sound and light show outside, which was too wild to watch for long. The vastness pressed in upon me, and I went to bed.

How could anyone help but believe in angry gods when the city is plunged into darkness, then lit up, in the middle of the night? The tree trunks of the eucalypts that fail to screen us from McDonald's were ghostly white, and behind them we could see white-light daggers hitting the city and the water beyond, and there were banging and crashing sounds like nothing in nature.

The storm passed. I woke at three in the morning, when the electric lights I had neglected to switch off suddenly came to life, pushing the by now gentle night back, beyond the little lighted city box I call home. And then I woke up this morning fearing for my seedlings. I had planted out pumpkin, cucumber, and melon. Would the snails, mobilized by rain, polish off the lot?

I was out there at dawn just as McDonald's opened. People were ordering their hotcakes at the drive-through, as I stood in my dressing gown and an old Akubra to protect me from the rain, with an empty yogurt container in hand, picking up the slugs and snails. My seedlings survived and are growing strongly. Once more, I feel like a successful gardener.

The rain is still falling tonight as I write this, but now it is kindly, plumping up the strawberries and sinking through the mulch. Today, I pulled out weeds with ease. The street trees all look as though someone has given them a tonic. The air is fresh and devoid of dust. Why does the weatherman apologize for rain? It is the greatest gift.

—

I miss having animals in my garden. A friend of mine has just bought chickens. She lives in a middle suburb, with room for a proper chicken pen — and proper is the word. Unlike me, my friend is an orderly, neat kind of person. She and her husband spent a week building a run, including burying the wire thirty centimeters down to foil the foxes that can, surprisingly, be found even in the heart of the city.

Then they purchased a coop in a flatpack from Bunnings and erected it inside the run. My friend does not like that old truism of farming — that if you have livestock you will eventually also have deadstock. She has, therefore, read every book there is to read on keeping backyard chickens, and is also the full bottle on Epsom salts baths, the planting of herbs for overall health, and every other matter.

I remember when I was the same, when I lived in the Blue Mountains. At times, I had up to thirty chickens, including our rooster, Vronsky. We did have deadstock. I buried the corpses by the roots of the fruit trees. There were a couple of distressing incidents involving foxes and quolls. I also had ducks.

But the most powerful experience was the day I picked up the goats. We wanted them not so much for milk, but to eat the great thickets of blackberries that grew on the edges of our block, and regenerated too fast for us to keep up with them. We sourced two adolescent goats from a farmer half an hour's drive away in the valley, and one day I went down and picked them up in the family station wagon.

It is only when you are sitting in a station wagon with two goats that you realize that up until this point in your life, 'goat' has been a theoretical concept. They were collared and tied for the journey, and, after some initial bleating, sat down and panted. Nevertheless, their goatiness was overwhelming. The smell of goat is, I think, the animal equivalent of the smell of pipe tobacco or cigars on a human. Goat smell is strong, acrid, uncompromising, and appealing, all at the same time. If it were a flavor, you would say that the seasoning was just right, because the taste would use up all of your tastebuds. There wouldn't be any redundant space on your tongue.

But it wasn't only the smell. It was their eyes, which were wide, and frightened, and full of deep anticipation of an unknown fate. And it was their faces, as individual as those of human beings, yet so animal — so totally unselfconscious and untroubled about being themselves. And it was their bodies, woolly and solid as barrels, which bumped and struggled with us as we put the collars on and got them tied up. During that half-hour car trip, the word 'goat' took on new significance for me. I had it in my head throughout, and by the end of the trip, it was in capital letters. GOAT.

I remember feeling quite ecstatic about the goats. In fact, I laughed aloud a few times on the Great Western Highway, which must have confirmed my insanity to the motorists around me. Two goats and one middle-aged woman, in a family wagon.

When we got home, we took the goats to their shed, and they spent the rest of the day standing around nervously. It was three days before they really began to eat. I was worried at first, but considered that for them, the experience of being in the station wagon with me would have been the equivalent of being kidnapped by aliens, and transported in a spaceship to an unfamiliar planet.

The goats ate the blackberries, and lived well but for a temporary attack of footrot during a wet winter — which saw me sliding around in the mud trying to paint their hooves with some purple solution purchased from the vet. They made me so happy. They gave me such perspective. Goats and chickens are so utterly themselves.

I have been looking at the lightwell between my house and that of the neighbor. It is currently the home to many weeds, a bit of self-seeded parsley, and the gas hot-water heater. Could we fit a couple of bantams in there? I asked my neighbor, and she vetoed the idea.

The rats and the worms in the compost heap will, for the moment, remain my only livestock.

~

My daughter asked me yesterday why King Edward potatoes are so called. I was busy scrubbing a set of them in preparation for roasting. I don't grow potatoes in my garden. I lack the room to make any kind of sensible crop, but I shop at the market's specialty potato store, where they know the difference between a King Edward, a Pink Eye, and a Kipfler. Most supermarkets only stock a couple of varieties — usually the sturdy Sebago, and the worthy all-purpose Pontiac. Or you can buy things called 'brushed potatoes', which could be anything at all.

My daughter had observed me making my choices, and now she wanted to know more.

We speculated that perhaps King Edward liked them, in which case he must have been a sensible, well-grounded man who appreciated a nice fluffy baked potato and a decent crisp chip. Once my daughter had gone, I thought further. Which King Edward? If it was the abdicating King Edward, then it made me wonder how the stick-thin Mrs Simpson could ever have led him astray. I think it was Mrs Simpson who said you could never be too thin. Clearly, she was not a potato woman. Perhaps there is a variety of celery named after her.

~

Last week, I visited one of the gardens of my growing up. Perhaps that is putting it a bit high. It was really the garden of my early adulthood — a time when I showed absolutely no interest in putting things into the soil and watching them grow. The garden is in a small Riverland town in South Australia. It was and is the garden of my first lover. When I first came to this house to stay, there was no garden — just hard stone and sand under a severe sun.

My friend used to dig all his household rubbish into the ground in the hope of creating soil. It worked after a fashion. I think he found an earthworm or two. But things really turned around when, somehow, gardening discovered him. One day, his garden was just a place to hang the washing. The next, it was a Big Project.

Within a few years, he was producing nearly all his own fruit and vegetables, and his conversation was almost entirely to do with the soil and the plants that supported him. He took pride in having something from his garden to eat at all times of year, and explored varieties of fruit that bore late and early. Buying fruit offended him. Having grown all the easy things, he attempted the difficult. For months, we tipped all tea-leaves into a particular spot, with the aim of making this powerfully limey soil acidic enough to grow camellias. This, at least, was a failure. But the garden was a glorious success.

My lover was a tidy man, most unlike me. He weeded. He kept records of what he had planted where, and whether or not it had worked. I remember long evenings, during which he would adjust the heads of his micro-sprinklers, changing this one to a faster rate, that one to a slower, depending on whether the plant concerned looked like it was getting enough.

He did proud and fussy things with the produce of his garden, like cutting fresh flowers every day, and cutting the pumpkin into neat squares for steaming. He gave some of his produce away, but his main aim in gardening was to produce enough for himself, and his guests, which included me. He was a self-contained man, in gardening as in many other things.

The garden is still beautiful today, but my friend died many years ago, when my children were young. These days, his widow does most of the weeding and harvesting, but the design he made so many years ago persists — a reminder of youth and hope, and a time when he gardened while I lounged in a hammock reading books, and having the sorts of epiphanies that come almost daily when one is young, in love, and leisure-rich. The view from his verandah is so imprinted on my memory that over all these years, I have been able to call it accurately to mind at any moment. I could map out every plant, tell you the history of every fruit tree, and the smell of every flower.

~

Yesterday, I was talking to someone about the habit of reflection, and how I feared giving it up. What would happen if I ceased to reflect on, and feel bad about, all the times I snap at the children? How messy would the garden be if I didn't occasionally feel guilty about not putting in the work to achieve my springtime ambitions? And what sort of writer would I be if I ever allowed myself to feel happy with my work?

The friend with whom I was discussing these things made an observation: that there is a difference between reflecting on one's actions, and criticizing them. Quite banal, really, in its obviousness, but it had power, because it has altered the person I have been today. I have worked at catching every piece of self-criticism, and stopping it. I am quite capable, of course, of kicking myself for kicking myself, and that is a hard one to catch, but I have tried.

I write about gardening partly to take the scariness away. So many gardening writers assume their audience has unlimited skill and time and money. As a result, I know, many people who would love to get their hands dirty instead shy away from mucking about with plants and soil. So it is odd to confess that I, too, get caught up in the lie that perfection is achievable and desirable. We need to be rescued from counsels of perfection. Or at least, I do.

At the moment, I have to contain my enthusiasm because for the first time a member of my family is showing an interest in gardening. My number two stepdaughter, an integral part of the family shrubbery, has dug up part of the backyard of her rented house, and has sought my advice. She has never gardened before. I have lent her all my books — a trolley-load — and today went with her to Bunnings.

My stepdaughter is an accountant, and a very precise person. We are good friends partly because in many ways we are opposites. I well remember sweeping a floor with her some years ago. I was wandering hither and thither with the broom, darting at bits of dust and detritus, whereas she was covering her area in systematic stripes.

So she has already made it clear that she wants to garden in the correct way, with neat rows of carrots, brassicas, and so forth — not all willy-nilly like me. Nevertheless, she seeks my guidance.

So we just wandered around the aisles of Bunnings, with me imparting bits of knowledge such as: don't plant peas next to members of the onion family; mix blood and bone with potash in proportions of ten to one for a complete garden fertilizer; and don't plant carrots near where you have dug in fresh manure, or they will fork, and fail to give you a decent root, so to speak.

I realized in about aisle 35, as she dithered over the decision on a compost bin, that she was feeling quite stressed. All this advice. It was too much. What was the correct way to plant? Would she manage it?

'You know,' I said, 'that if you bung things in the soil most of them will grow?'

She looked at me doubtfully.

I paused, then said: 'I guess you aren't going to be comfortable with the idea that there is no correct way? That it's up to you.'

'No', she said. 'I am not comfortable with that AT ALL.'

And we laughed as we drove back to her place, the compost bin teetering in the back seat.

AUTUMN

About a year ago, I planted a vine called a Happy Wanderer against the back fence in the lane that lies between the rear of my home and the McDonald's carpark. I hoped it would grow to screen what I call my Andy Warhol view — multiple burgers and golden arches on the illuminated drive-through menu, all aglow and clearly visible from the windows of my living room.

I chose this species of vine (*Hardenbergia Violacea*, for those who like to know such things) because in my previous Blue Mountains abode it went nuts in the harshest conditions, and cloaked all kinds of ugliness, including an old shipping container I used as a garden shed, and a rusty, half-buried water tank that sheltered my goats from the elements. It was a lovely plant, carrying spear-shaped leaves and, at the end of winter, blue flowers that hung in lobes. I thought it was indestructible, and so imported another example of the species to this inner-urban, brick-paved chapter of my life.

This time, though, the Happy Wanderer did not live up to its name. For some weeks it sat passively, not putting on any new growth. It had come from the garden nursery complete with a little white plastic trellis, to imply that it would soon be climbing. I carefully wound its two tendrils around the trellis to give it some encouragement. Nothing happened, and after a month, it died.

I put the failure down to the towering gum trees that McDonald's planted on the other side of the fence many years ago, as part of a settlement in a planning dispute in which the neighbors objected to an extension of opening hours. Under the terms of the settlement, McDonald's were allowed to open at 6.00 a.m. and trade until midnight, and we were given money to pay for double-glazing. McDonald's also planted the trees. They grew rapidly, and were completely ineffective, leaving bare trunks and a clear view of McDonald's at eye level, and tossing messy heads of leaves far above the Golden Arches. They sucked the water out of the soil for meters around.

This, I concluded, together with my culpable neglect and general incompetence, was why my Happy Wanderer had carked it. I am sure it really was dead. I checked. All through winter, and then through a baking summer, the corpse of the Wanderer reproached me. Dead tendrils clung to the silly white plastic trellis. I was too lazy to pull it out, and I didn't give it a drop of water. Instead, I planted a Nellie Kellie passionfruit, which seemed to do rather better than the Happy Wanderer.

Gardeners know that there are two times of year when life seems particularly stubborn. One is spring, of course. The other is autumn. In the autumn flush, plants that sulked through the heat suddenly put on a surge. The lavender puts out new shoots.

The citrus trees are tipped with russet-colored new growth. The gardening world briefly stands on tiptoes before hunkering down for winter.

Yet I was shaken when, as I pushed my bike down the back lane, I saw a leaf on the Happy Wanderer. I was sure at first that it was some other weed, simply growing on the bones of my failed attempt at screening. I crouched down and traced the stem with my finger. It looked like a Happy Wanderer leaf. But how could it be? It had been three-quarters of a year since there had been any signs of life. And yet, there it was. Resurrection. It had come back to life, somehow surviving the bone-dry dirt, the lack of care, the baking temperatures through summer. Each day since then, there has been a new leaf. It isn't growing fast, but it has reached the top of the little white trellis, and last week I spent some time fooling around with clout nails, hammer, and chicken wire to erect something more substantial to support its stubborn growth. I am not sure I am allowed to do this. The lane, after all, belongs to the council. The fence belongs to McDonald's. I am trespassing. Yet I feel justified, if not impelled. This is, after all, a matter of life and death.

As I messed around, hitting my thumbs as often as the nails, I found myself thinking about Friedrich Nietzsche, who wrote a book called *How to Philosophize with a Hammer* (truly, that was its name, although it also was called *Twilight of the Idols*). At first, I was just thinking that I might achieve more with philosophy and a hammer than I was with the trellis. But then I remembered that it was in this book that Nietzsche wrote some much quoted and misquoted words — the phrase for which he is perhaps best known. He said 'what does not kill me makes me stronger'. Nietzsche is not my favorite philosopher, and I'd be prepared to bet he wasn't a gardener, despite the fact that he has a great deal to say about nature. Nature, he said was 'boundlessly extravagant, boundlessly indifferent, without purpose or consideration, without pity or justice, at once fruitful and barren'. He also thought of nature as female, and he didn't like women much.

But that idea of adversity making one stronger — it isn't always true. For example, aphids and cucumbers. My cucumber plants had survived a severe aphid outbreak during the autumn flush, thanks to my homemade garlic potion, and a daily regime of crushing the aphids with my fingers. But the plants were much weakened. No super-cucumber emerged from adversity. I'll be lucky to get any cucumbers at all before the cold brings things to an end.

But the Happy Wanderer? How had it survived? Without the benefits of any photosynthesis or other means of support, its roots must have twined their away around those of the monster gums, burrowed under the McDonald's drive-through bitumen, travelled far, and found water. I don't know if the Happy Wanderer will ever block my view of drivers ordering their thickshakes and fries. I no longer really care. As I coddle my weakened cucumbers, spraying them each morning, smearing my fingers with aphid corpses, I can see the Happy Wanderer (what an anodyne name) ascending tendril by tendril. I hardly dare to water it in case my care disrupts some crucial element of the miracle. I am a little frightened of it. It doesn't need me at all.

This week, I have been reflecting on my family. It is a rather haphazard array of people, a cherished side effect of a life that has not gone to plan. I have four adult stepchildren, two teenage children of my own, two ex-partners (parents of the stepchildren, two apiece), and two step-grandchildren. Then there is the ex-girlfriend of one of my stepsons. She, too, is family.

Often, talking to people who don't know me well, I feel I should draw a diagram to explain how these individuals are related to me, and to each other. It is not so much a family tree as a family shrubbery. At times, I feel very sad that my two long-term relationships did not last, but while the evidence suggests I am not very good at marriage, I have proved rather excellent at family. My house has become the central node of the family shrubbery. Many people have keys. Many people who have no blood relationship come to Sunday dinner, and regard each other as brothers, sisters, and cousins. It's a tangle, but I am rather proud of it. As well, my own children benefit from having half-brothers and half-sisters, and stepbrothers and stepsisters, who are young enough to be cool, but old enough to be mentors.

For people in their twenties and early thirties, settling down is a sometime thing. So it is that quite often some subset of the shrubbery will be moving furniture from one home to another. Tables, chairs, fridges, washing machines, and baby clothes circulate between us, travelling around the suburbs as need requires. In this constant movement, my house and garden is a fixed point — a place where items are stored or dropped. It helps that I have a loft. Up there are stored the garbage bags of baby clothes, the high chair that one child has grown out of, and another not yet grown in to. There are three stands for Christmas trees — the property of three different households. There is a home brewing kit, a portable clothesline, and more sleeping bags and suitcases than we are ever likely to use.

So it was that yesterday I was standing with stepson number two in the no-man's land of the back lane. We were, once again, loading stuff carried down from the loft on to the back of a rented ute. There was a pause while we waited for my ex-partner to arrive and help. Standing in the weak autumn sunshine, among the fallen leaves and discarded hamburger wrappings, I found myself pointing out the plants against the McDonald's fence. I had narrowly avoided destroying them as we clumsily backed the ute.

I showed him the miraculous Happy Wanderer, now living up to its name. Then I pointed out its companions. 'That is parsley, and that is coriander, but it's dying. And that is a passionfruit vine,' I said.

He did a double take. 'Passionfruit grows on a VINE?' he said. My stepson is not a gardener.

'Yes.'

'How?'

'Well, it flowers, and then it sets fruit.'

'But isn't it too heavy? How does it stay up when it's carrying fruit?' He was truly astonished.

'Just like a cucumber or any other vine.'

He did another double take. 'Cucumbers grow on a VINE?'

So I showed him the wiry tendrils the passionfruit vine has thrown around the trellis. It has grown astonishingly well — more than a meter during the autumn flush.

Its tendrils are like green springs, winding multiple times in perfect coils to lock the plant tight against its support.

My stepson brushed his finger against the tendrils. 'How does it know where to put them?' he said quietly. He is a vehement atheist, so I did not attempt an answer. Not that I had one. Although, given half a chance I would have shamed myself with vague talk of a way of things, an instinct for growth, a universal miracle best described as things growing almost no matter what, and life continuing in messy fashion no matter what plans we make, and the wonder of unintended consequences. But I had the sense not to say any of that. After all, we were standing amid the rubbish from McDonald's, loading furniture onto a ute.

There were some passionfruit tendrils — a lighter green than those locked around the trellis — that were reaching out to the lane. 'They don't all know where to go,' I said, pulling out the spiral of an unanchored example, and letting it snap back on itself.

He found a tendril that was less than completely regular in its spiral grip on the trellis. 'Well,' he said, in a tone of satisfaction. 'It stuffed that one up.' He meant, of course, that it was not perfect.

We had a little longer to wait, and he took a look at my compost bin. The worms had climbed through a layer of dead leaves to feed on the latest bin of kitchen waste. There was a cluster of them nestled in an eggshell, feeding on the remains of the white. We contemplated them quietly, our heads bowed together.

Then my ex arrived, and we packed up the back of the ute, and drove out of the lane and around the suburb, delivering stuff to its latest home.

~

About three years ago, a friend of mine moved house. Because he had no room for it, he gave me a small, gray succulent plant in one of those raffia-style hanging baskets.

I am not a fan of succulents, nor of raffia baskets. I can easily justify my dislike of raffia. For a start, it rots. And, when it isn't rotting, it fails to hold moisture through the heat of summer. I have never before successfully grown anything in a woven pot or basket of any kind, and I always suspect that the gardening magazines that show gaily flowering petunias and the like in hanging baskets have whipped them up just for the photo opportunity, and that within weeks they will be barren.

My dislike of succulents is harder to justify. They take no care, grow in places where nothing else survives, and look interesting enough. Perhaps I don't like them because they are, in a suburban garden, almost entirely useless. You can't eat them, sit under them, or use them for lawn. They seem an indulgence. But it is more than that. There is something about their fleshy juiciness that repels me. When they flower, they look like aliens. I have been known to talk to my plants, but if I spoke to a cactus I would suspect my sanity. They are not of my world.

Growing succulents is a bit like having a stick insect for a pet, or a boring pen friend as a correspondent. It makes you wonder why you bother.

Not wanting to offend my friend, I put the hanging basket containing his succulent down beside the yellow recycling bin in my front yard, and said I would find a proper place for it later. Then I forgot about it, or in any case could not be bothered. I thought it would die, or at least sulk uselessly until I got up the will to kill it. I half hoped someone would steal it.

Instead, it thrived. The thick gray leaves grew larger. Soon there were more of them flowing over the sides of the hanging basket. The basket disintegrated but the succulent grew stronger, and now the damn thing is enormous. Every fortnight, I extract the yellow bin from its tight spot between succulent and gate, and manoeuvre it out on the kerb for collection. Accidentally-on-purpose, I run over a bit of the succulent. I trample on it. I snap off branches. I mutter at it under my breath. When I put the wheelie bin back, I ram it against the plant. Take that, I think. I wish it death. The leaves snap and squish in their crisp, liquidy fashion. It takes damage, dropping limbs and bleeding clear sap.

Yet within two days it has collected itself, and, like a tiresome acquaintance who won't take a hint, seems even happier to be in my life. Now it overruns a fair bit of my precious space, taking up room that could be occupied by coriander or carrots. It has put out tall, spindly flower heads that droop pale-orange bell-like appendages.

I admit to grudging admiration.

Last weekend, I found that this triffid-like thing has rooted in a number of places, making new plants in virgin soil. I took out the secateurs and cut it back. Normally, when one cuts back woody plants, the secateurs making satisfying decisive incisions, promoting healthy new growth. This thing was barely cuttable. It gave way under the blade, squishy and malleable, and it bled everywhere.

I didn't take it all away. I want to see what it will do. Each evening, I look at its pale stumps, and imagine that it is looking back at me. What will it do? Die, or come back? I feel mean and guilty about my succulent. I don't like the person it causes me to become. This plant sees the nastiest things about me. It receives all the frustration and grumpiness I hide from others. I am not sure I want it to die. I hate it, but it is mine.

~

Right next to the hated succulent is one of the few unqualified success stories of my gardening since I came to the big city. It is my lavender — two big bushes, one English, one Italian. When I lived in near self-sufficiency in the Blue Mountains, I had a long lavender hedge. The soil up there in the mountains was thin, sandy, acid, and weak, and the lavender never thrived. Nevertheless, I loved lavender so much that I persisted. When the foxes killed my chickens, the corpses were buried near the roots of the lavender or the fruit trees to provide some nourishment. Each morning, I would brush against the plants to release their scent. Each autumn, I would clip back the scanty flowers, collect the prunings, and tie them in bundles for drying. There were never enough flowers to allow me to imitate those pictures in magazines of French provincial style, with great bundles of fragrant flowers strung from ceilings. But still, I dreamed.

When I moved to the city, I brought some clippings from that hedge, and when they rooted (in itself a small miracle), I planted them against the front wall of my house, under the bedroom window. Although the soil here also tends to acid, and lavender likes alkaline conditions, the plants took off. For the last three years I have had a *real* lavender hedge — fragrant, thick, and, at the end of summer, covered in flowers and bees.

Lavender needs to be cut back after flowering, or else it becomes what the gardening books refer to as 'leggy'. This means that the wooden trunks at the base of the plant spread outwards and upwards. Under the gray-green foliage and flowers there is a netherworld of dusty, cobwebby, dead leaves and twigs. In time, the trunks split, the flowers and leaves fall to the ground, and the plant goes from a thing of beauty to a gnarly nuisance. I am not a great pruner, but even I know that if my lavender is to continue to make me proud, I must cut back.

It hurts to do it, of course. The gardening books say to prune back hard after flowering, but a good lavender plant has never entirely finished flowering. There are always some fresh sentinel blue flowers standing erect among the dead-head remnants of the summer profusion. But one must cut back hard. The living must take its place among the dead.

So last weekend I got busy with my secateurs. I had, as usual, left it a little late and the lavender plants were already showing signs of the dreaded legginess. I had decided, in a moment of profound lack of self-knowledge, to try to shape the plant as a neat square hedge. I cut and trimmed and hacked, sneezing from the dust and dead leaves. I threw the trimmings over the fence on to the footpath, planning to gather them up later, tie them up in bunches, hang them in the porch to dry, and use them for potpourri and in lavender bags.

I must have been at it for about half an hour, and was nearly done when I turned around. There were more lavender clippings on the footpath than there was lavender still attached to the plant. The cuttings had piled up, spilling to the gutter, almost as high as the fence. There was far too much to fit in the compost bin. If I tied it all up in bundles and hung it in the porch, there wouldn't be room to get in the front door.

I have always resisted the blandishments of the council to get a green bin. Perhaps this is a hangover from my days of self-sufficiency on those thin, acid soils. In those days, when I had at least three compost heaps, taking organic matter off the premises seemed like a profound waste. What I wanted was humus, and lots of it. I couldn't get enough organic matter.

Now, in the city, I have room for only one large compost bin, but I still object to the idea of giving away organic matter to somebody else. On a few occasions, I have cadged space in my neighbor's green bin, but I try to save that for the really noxious weeds, such as oxalis and onion grass, that even ardent composters reject as ingredients. Otherwise I store clippings, cram them into the bin, or in some way endeavor to deal with them on the premises.

The lavender glut was clearly going to overwhelm me, and now my neighbors were beginning to smile testily as they were forced to step into the gutter to get past my house and its lavender overflow.

I began to gather it all up. I made three enormous bundles for myself, and hung them untidily in the porch — not so much French provincial as Australian birds' nest. The footpath was still overflowing, so I grabbed every bucket in the house, and crammed lavender into it. I lined them up against the fence, and put out a cardboard notice reading 'lavender, free to good home.'

It felt cheeky to fool people in to taking my garden rubbish, but that evening, as people made their way down to the takeaway restaurants on the main road, a surprising number of them carried home branches of lavender with their pizzas and burgers.

When I got up the next day, almost all the lavender was gone. It wasn't until I checked the mailbox that I realized one of my neighbors had left me something in return.

There was an envelope containing two folds of kitchen paper. Inside one were long seed pods, which, when rubbed between thumb and forefinger, yielded a scattering of hard black specks — rocket seeds. The other fold of kitchen paper contained dried-up yellow capsules. Sweetcorn seed. My unknown neighbor had left a note.

'Thanks for your generosity with the lavender. I am local. Here is something from my garden for you.'

~

My compost bin was falling apart. It is an Aerobin, the extra-expensive square type that is vermin-proof, with an internal chimney which, when it is working, keeps everything cooking and sweet without the need for turning. For nearly eight years it has served me well, but now it is sagging at the seams. The rats can get in, and the compost falls out.

Last weekend, in a frenzy of gardening, I put on my oldest gardening trousers and took the bin apart, digging out the compost ready for the garden bed. I intended to rebuild the compost bin once it was empty. I was halfway through the job when a turn of the shovel brought down a nest of half-a-dozen tiny baby rats — pink and hairless, with blind bulbous heads straining for a teat.

A very fat mother rat ran out under my feet a moment later. What to do?

Living in the inner suburbs, and right next to a McDonald's restaurant, I have long ago overcome my reservations about laying out rat bait. Either one does it, or one is overrun. But these were babies, right in front of me, and their mother had gone.

Some months ago, I cooked dinner for a friend who is a hard-line vegan. I find such meals a challenge. Vegetarian is easy. We often have meatless meals. But this time I found myself constantly wanting to reach for the forbidden. Fish sauce. Chicken stock. Cream and milk. All of it, as my friend would say, involving death and exploitation.

We got through with garlic mushrooms (minus the parmesan) and pea soup (on vegetable stock), with good bread, and cream on the side for those who wanted to add it. When it came to desert, I offered fruit with honey, only to find that the product of bees is also off the vegan list.

'But bees make honey anyway, don't they?' I asked, and got a small lecture on the cruelty of stealing it from them, smoking the bees — all the nastiness of honey factory-farming. A few days later, my friend sent links to websites that backed her up.

I was impressed, even awed, by her consistency.

And now I, the honey-eater, stood shovel in hand over the hairless baby rats. I knew I couldn't raise them, and of course I didn't really want to. I try to get rid of rats. They make me shudder. I wasn't sure if the mother would come back if I simply left them. And even if she did, why would I preserve the rats when I also laid rat bait?

I thought about burying them in the garden with the compost — but burying them alive was surely not a kindness. It was cowardice.

I went inside, made a cup of tea, and drank it slowly, watching from the window, not knowing if I was hoping for mother rat to come back. She didn't.

After half an hour I went back out and saw the little pink

hairless babies still straining blindly. I stood transfixed. It was cruel to leave them like that.

I brought the shovel down on them — once, twice, thrice — and killed them outright, before shovelling the compost on the garden.

That night, I didn't sleep.

And the next day, I attempted to rebuild the compost bin so that it didn't bulge and sag, so that it would once again be rat-proof. It didn't work.

Then I bought gaffer tape, and tried to stick it all together, blocking the holes. The next morning, I found the rats had eaten through the tape, and were once again in the compost heap, doubtless nesting. More pink little babies to come. More murder.

It was one of my readers who provided me with the solution. He told me to go to Bunnings and buy the big industrial strength straps that truck drivers use to tie down their loads. I looped these around the compost bin, and ratcheted them tight. The bin was drawn tight, the holes closed up. It no longer sagged.

Then I lay rat bait nearby. I am hoping this will be enough.

I still eat honey. I am not going to stop.

~

Let a parsnip go to seed in your garden, and you will have parsnips forever — which means, I suppose, that you will never starve. But then you wouldn't anyway. The supermarket is after all just around the corner, and McDonald's is at the back fence. But suppose we were peasants. We would be grateful then for parsnips, and Jerusalem artichokes, and potatoes, and all those other unglamorous, sweet, fart-producing root vegetables that were once like money in the bank: a bulwark against desperation.

When parsnip seed is very fresh, it sprouts easily. When you buy stale seed, everything is hard work. Parsnip seed that is more than a week or two old is surely one of the most frustrating seeds of all. Getting my one parsnip to grow from three whole packets of Yates seed took lots of work, in spite of all the little foil envelopes and assurances of quality. It seems to be beyond some seed companies to admit that they are not all-powerful, and that some seed is meant to be planted when very fresh, not collected, packaged, priced, and distributed through shops.

Two springs ago, I mollycoddled my three packets of shop-bought parsnip seed. I covered the row with hessian to ensure the soil stayed moist, and watered through the cloth to make sure I didn't wash everything away. When the first feathery frond of my single parsnip plant showed above the soil, I was vigilant. Snails and slugs were ruthlessly murdered. Birds were deterred. Rats were baited. This baby was precious, and could not be allowed to fail.

Finally, the parsnip was established, the long white taproot pushing down, and I could afford to relax. I left it entirely alone, and watched through summer as the root grew from a thin white finger to a great woody pole. The top went from delicate green leaves, suitable for salad (young parsnip tops are wonderful in salad), to a huge stem, taller than me, topped with yellow flowers and drooping over the neighbor's fence. As summer died, so did the flowers and then, there was my seed — far more than three packets full. More than I have room for. I had parsnip seed galore. I picked the flower heads and sprinkled them over the garden, and very quickly wished I had been more discriminating, because now parsnips grow like weeds in my garden. They are everywhere.

As weeds go, parsnips are very good. Parsnips don't take much out of the soil, and they form a canopy that keeps other weeds out. After rain, they come out easily, leaving you with clear ground nicely dug by their roots. They are the most undemanding, humble of vegetables. Spoil them with fresh manure and fertilizer and they go all silly, forking and twisting and splitting, and making themselves quite unsuitable for the pot. Sow them in ground that grew a more demanding crop the previous season, and they grow straight and true.

These reflections have been provoked because I have just been pulling them up to make way for more spinach and brassica seedlings. This is a preparation for our winter eating.

Parsnips straight out of the ground look unimpressive — pale and dirty, like an old derro's legs. But put them into the pot and they are the most romantic of vegetables, more aromatic than a carrot, and taking in butter like sponge cake takes in sherry. As a result of my clearing the ground, I have more parsnips than I want to eat, even though I plan to make parsnip and bacon soup with parsley and cream. What wonderful things root vegetables are. What great aromas, colors, and tastes are created down there below the soil, here in the shadow of the city. What would the world be without garlic, and yams, and sweet potato, and ordinary potato, and carrots, and turnips, and onions. All are created out of sight, mechanisms for extracting nutrition and water from soil.

Here in the bright, washing-drying, sunny up-world, I find myself giving thanks for all root vegetables, but for parsnips in particular.

—

I don't have room to grow pumpkins. Really, I don't. Nevertheless, I do it. It almost never goes well. They trail out of the pots on the verandah, and drag the plant out by the roots as they grow. More often, the aphids get them first. But this year, through some accident of sunshine and moisture, I have managed to grow a pumpkin vine on the roof — its roots in one of my biggest, deepest polystyrene boxes. For the last few weeks, three pumpkins have been ripening on the roof, lying near the gutter like little earthbound suns.

Pumpkins are best harvested when the vine has died, which means autumn — the time of traditional harvest festivals. This last week, we have had a couple of genuinely cold nights, and you can almost see the check, the pause, and the beginning of preparations for winter. The whole garden seems to be stilled, and the pumpkin vines wilted a bit from the cold. Time to harvest. I cut the pumpkins from the vine, carried them into the kitchen, and bundled the rest of the plant into the compost.

When lack of rain, or lack of nutrition, or lack of sunlight, or lack of warmth makes raising plants from the ground a difficult thing to do, it is hard to remember that nature is not an economic rationalist. Nature believes in hedging bets, in waste and superfluity.

I remembered this as I cut into those pumpkins. Inside that horny yellow skin was the familiar egg-yolk yellow, and a wealth of white, slithery pumpkin seeds. They spilled out onto the chopping board, thin and wet, sliding over each other, sticking to fingers and knives, resisting all attempts to get them into the rubbish bin. Even after tea, when roast pumpkin and roast chicken had been eaten and cleared away, I was still finding pumpkin seeds under the chopping board and in the bottom of the dishwasher. It made me wonder how the purveyors of pumpkin seed make a living, when we must all throw so many of the things away.

If every one of these made a new pumpkin vine, I thought, there wouldn't be room in the garden for anything else. If I grew them on the roof, it would collapse. As it is, I always find the compost heap grows a few volunteer plants.

The truth is that not all of them would grow. As in the parable, some would fall by the wayside, some would be choked by briars, some would fall on stony ground, spring up and be withered by the sun, and only a chosen few — cosseted on my roof, perhaps — would grow to maturity.

But the time of pumpkin growing is over, and we are on the way to winter — that season of mean struggle in the vegetable patch. Now is the time for darker-green, frost-tolerant leaves — slow-growing spinach, and rocket that is at its best in autumn, lest it bolt to seed.

There is no avoiding the fact that the vegetable garden is now preparing for its winter sulk, and I am struggling to delay the day that the brassicas become our staple vegetables. I keep telling myself there is nothing wrong with cabbage, but one cannot be English (as I am, by birth) without being burdened by race memories of soggy, gray vegetable matter cooking in liters of water for far too long, and being served under the name of cabbage. There are, it must be admitted, compensatory race memories of cauliflower cheese with a crispy breadcrumb top, but even this cannot wipe out the centuries of suffering inflicted on my people through overcooked cabbage.

Yesterday, I prepared a casserole, with all the vegetables picked from my few square meters of soil. I sallied forth under a drizzly sky, and considered what vegetables were available. Parsnips, of course. And then there was the celery, which grows leggy and leafy because it is light-deprived, but which tastes fine in any case. There were also a few green tomatoes hanging on to the withering vine like babies to skirts, and some silverbeet, also self-seeded, to add green bulk.

All this, and I hadn't even thought of touching the brassicas in the fridge. The inevitable cabbage is forestalled for a while. So, too, the trip to the supermarket. It will come, though. It will come.

There are compensations to the approach of winter. The smell of a frosty evening. The slower growth of weeds. An end to the season of lawn-mowing — not that I have a lawn. Nevertheless, in my tiny patch of soil here in the suburbs, there is a sense of descent, of laying down stores, of girding one's metaphorical loins for a trial.

When I open the door to the pantry, there is another golden-yellow pumpkin, and in spring, I will plant a couple of its slithery white seeds in another polystyrene box on the roof.

~

Call it a cliché, or call it an archetype. The rounds of the seasons give us one of the reliable metaphors of human storytelling. We know the deal: hope comes in spring, ripeness in summer, sadness in autumn, and stoicism or death in winter. Yet these days, only gardeners and farmers are in touch with this pattern. The supermarket robs us of the rhythm of story.

In any case, modern life is not as neat as a seasonal metaphor. This week, I finished a book. It is rather like recovering from a long illness. Suddenly, there is time and energy once again. I can garden without feeling that I should be at my desk. I can stare out of the window without each breath being tinged with guilt. For a brief golden period, I can enjoy the feeling of *having written* without the anxiety of *having to write.* I am always deeply suspicious of those who claim to love writing. I hate it. What I love is the feeling that comes *before* the project, when all is possibility and potential, and the feeling that comes afterwards, which is pure relief. The bit in between is agony, guilt, and anxiety. When one is mid-book, even weeding and edge clipping become infinitely attractive.

In any case, to celebrate my temporary freedom from performance anxiety, I decided to plant daffodil bulbs. It is late to be doing this. Planting bulbs — garlic or spring flowers — is something one normally does earlier in autumn. But in April I was still mid-project, and if I had allowed myself to indulge in any of the pleasurable bits of gardening, the writing work would never have been done. Gardening is such sweet procrastination. It was George Bernard Shaw, I think, who once said that vegetable growing is the only unquestionably useful thing a person can do. What is writing compared to that?

Liberated from guilt, I went to Bunnings wielding my $50 gift token, a remnant of summer and Christmas. I bought a big, shiny, red outdoor pot, and a little net bag of bulbs. Outside on the verandah, my fingers red from cold, I poured in potting mix laced with home-made compost. My compost comes out of the big, green Aerobin that takes up a square meter of the backyard. I like to reflect on how it reflects what is happening in the house. So this compost, being the product of a household in which a book is being written, contained more than the usual amount of tea-leaves and coffee grounds.

I stirred the mix together and watered it, then ripped open the net bag of bulbs to find that they already had spears of green emerging from their brown papery skins. They were ahead of time, and I was behind time. They were going in to the soil just in time. I buried them with the merest tip of green showing above the soil.

Meanwhile, I have been struggling with the coriander. What is it with this herb? It has to be the most difficult of plants. Sow it in summer, and it gives you a few leaves then goes spindly and to seed. Plant it in winter, and it grows so slowly you hardly dare snip it.

So I am planting lots now, in autumn, because coriander is

one of the miracle herbs, capable of rendering any meal fragrant and exotic. I have planted it in the back lane next to the miracle Happy Wanderer. I have planted it in a polystyrene box on my neighbor's roof, and I have planted it between the morose broccoli in the strip of earth between the front of my house and the street.

Of these three sites, only one is working. The coriander is doing well with the broccoli, growing low and lush. Meanwhile, it is languishing in the lane, and dying on the roof. Light, water, and liquid fertilizer make no difference.

I consulted the gardening books for hints as to why this might be, and learned that coriander is a very deep-rooted plant. The feathery leaves at the top are merely the fluffiest, most trivial, and easiest to access part of the plant. The root can reach up to a meter underground, long, white and fleshy, like an elongated parsnip, or an essential ingredient in some witches' brew. The root can be harvested as a vegetable in its own right, and ground up or steamed. Shallow pots and my polystyrene boxes simply hadn't given it enough room.

A real gardener would have consulted the books before planting, rather than after, but that, too, would have felt too much like procrastination while the Big Book was underway. Scattering seeds willy-nilly, on the other hand, could be excused as not real work, and therefore a permissible distraction.

'Buy some,' said my daughter. 'It comes in a tube at the supermarket these days.' I told her that wasn't the same. Meanwhile, my stepson, cutting sandwiches on my kitchen bench the other day, asked if I had bought tomatoes, since he could find none in the fridge.

I realized how far I had drifted from the normal concerns of the non-gardening world when I replied that I had not, because they were not in season. Who would buy the artificially ripened, flavorless mini-cannonballs that pass for tomatoes at this time of year? This is the verge of winter, I said. It is the time for chutney, and things pickled, dried, salted, and put aside.

He stared at me and left for the supermarket.

Meanwhile, I put the kettle on and made another cup of tea, and gazed out at my red pot of daffodil bulbs. The tiny, brave green tips were a fraction higher above the soil than when I planted them. They are signs of faith in kinder times to come, even though a long winter lies between now and spring.

During the coming season, my writing life will lie fallow. What a sense of possibility there is in the lack of a Big Project. At this distance, if feels as though I could write anything, precisely because I know I will write nothing.

By spring, I will once again be locked in that sad, obsessive space in which each day of work feels like an exercise in incompetence, and I scatter seed in a mood somewhere between desperation and despair, or perhaps in sheer stubborn hope that despite me, things will grow.

WINTER

Ancient mythologies are full of winter as a time of retreat and sadness. Pluto, ruler of the infernal regions, reaches out his power. Sap is withdrawn from leaves, and they fall. Animals hibernate. Winter is a time of gray and black. The season is a metaphor for death, but also for hope, because we all know that spring will come. All these descriptions and metaphors, of course, are tied up with the Northern Hemisphere, and a life very different in time and geography from my inner-urban professionalism. The street trees drop their leaves, the catalogues in the letterbox are full of advertisements for heating and insulation, and the shops hold seasonal sales. But nobody stores away nuts and pickles. Nobody salts meat for long keeping, or worries about making it through to spring.

As a gardener, I find there is much to look forward to in winter. Is there any more powerful passage of the Bible than the assertion, 'To everything there is a season, and a time to every purpose under the heaven: A time to be born, and a time to die; a time to plant and a time to pluck up that which is planted'?

One of the things I do in winter is pluck up, not the things that have been planted, but the things that keep on bloody planting themselves. Weeds, in other words. In winter, things stop growing, and so for a few short months I have the illusion that I am a real gardener, able to keep up with and control growth. I weed things, and they stay weeded. For once, despite shorter days and longer nights, I appear to be in control.

It is also the time for infrastructure projects — for building and planning, erecting trellises and making garden beds, and doing all those other things that help to make a garden more than a collection of plants. Once upon a time in England, a garden was understood to be part of what it was to be civilized. It was the space between the house and the countryside — an intermediary between the wilderness and the world of the antimacassar, at once a tribute to nature, and evidence of human control over it. Whole generations of European landscape-gardeners built their careers around different ideas of humankind's place in the natural world, and the transition from wilderness to civilization.

In my case, the garden is the buffer and point of transition between home and the urban wilderness, and my infrastructure projects reflect this: the clumsy trellis between me and the McDonald's carpark, the thick jasmine on the boundary with my neighbor at the front that helps us to remain clearly separate households, even though we live close enough to hear each other open our cereal boxes in the morning.

Although my space is limited, I find myself longing for that most basic means of defying the seasons — a greenhouse. I like being able to pick my own tomatoes in winter, or at least early spring, when those hard green things in the supermarket are priced at several king's ransoms. Dr Faust is meant to have sold his soul to the devil in return for a long life during which he had every pleasure possible. I seem to remember that one of these soul-priced pleasures was strawberries in the middle of winter. In these days of irradiation and deep freezes, there is nothing special about strawberries. Nevertheless, I suspect that we have done a worse deal than Dr Faust. We have sold our souls for flavorless tomatoes in mid-winter, and we don't even enjoy them.

In my previous gardening life, I had the space and the freedom to build myself a greenhouse, and thus made my own less dramatic Faustian pact. The decision was prompted largely by a design I saw in two gardening magazines more or less simultaneously. I had no money for a proper greenhouse, but this method was cheap and simple.

You got garden stakes, the magazines said, and drove them into the ground in two rows at intervals of about a meter and a half. Then you got black polypipe of the sort used for garden irrigation, cut lengths, and threaded the ends over the garden stakes, like gloves over fingers, to form hoops between the two rows. Then you got tough plastic sheeting, and spread it over the lot. Bingo, a cheap greenhouse. The gardening magazines said a small version should cost about $50, and take no more than a few hours to build.

It wasn't quite so simple. First, I decided I wanted a bigger greenhouse, so more plastic and more pipe was needed. Then I was told that star pickets would be better than gardening stakes, and star pickets aren't cheap. Then, because the star pickets were thick, I needed bigger polypipe to fit over them. Eventually, I dragged back from various hardware shops and agricultural suppliers about $400 worth of materials, and at the end of a weekend of work I had my greenhouse. The whole thing looked rather like a giant condom, but in it I grew my tomatoes in the depths of a Blue Mountains winter, with temperatures outside well below zero at nighttime.

Now I am trying to work out how to have a greenhouse on my little inner-urban plot. There is simply no room. Instead, I am collecting soft drink bottles, cutting out the bottoms and putting them over my seedlings. I won't have home-grown tomatoes in winter, but I will preserve the last of the autumn, and get a head-start on spring.

~

People used to worry about how to get rid of their hair and toenail clippings, because they were thought to be useful for witchcraft. Sir James Frazer wrote in *The Golden Bough* — that great exploration of human spiritual belief — that many human cultures included the belief that people could be bewitched using any 'severed portion of the person'.

The Marquesan Islanders believed that if a sorcerer buried someone's hair with the correct rites, the victim would waste away. His life could be saved by discovering and digging up the buried hair. Maori sorcerers buried people's hair or toe clippings, and chanted over them. As they decayed, the owner began to die. In the Tyrol, witches were supposed to use cut or combed-out hair to make hailstones and thunderstorms. The Romans apparently shared some of this belief. On board ships, nobody was allowed to cut their hair or nails for fear of bringing bad weather.

I know these things because I am a compost enthusiast, and this is the kind of funny knowledge you pick up, because human hair also makes an excellent compost ingredient. Some of the gardening bloggers I follow — those of the more witchy-poo pagan school of thought — nevertheless reject the idea of human hair as compost for fear they will do injury to the owner of the material.

My son doesn't like having his hair cut. Unfortunately, he does not have the kind of hair that hangs loose, containable into a ponytail or otherwise able to be worn in a cool fashion. He has a thick, wiry mop that, left to itself, grows out in an ever increasing mat that makes his head look twice its natural size.

He sees no problem with this. He procrastinates about cutting it until past the point where everyone in the family is telling him it needs doing — even number one stepson, who is regarded as cool and therefore gets listened to when the rest of us are ignored.

My son also resents having to spend money on a hairdresser, and I dole out pocket money in large amounts, out of which the children are meant to pay for their own clothes and grooming. In theory, this teaches them budgeting and financial management. In my son's case, it seems to result in self-neglect. But this week, the combination of family pressure and an empty wallet meant that he accepted his sister's offer of a home haircut.

It was a bit like pruning. Once she had started, it was hard to stop. Wads of hair fell over his shoulders and across the floor, and still his head resembled a mop. She went further. She rediscovered his ears. His forehead was exposed. He began to look human, even respectable. Finally the job was done, and there was enough hair on the floor to stuff a pillow, which I suggested. This notion was rejected with disgust.

I didn't tell him what I was going to do next. Later that evening, I went down to the compost bin carrying a bucket brimful of bits of my son, lifted the lid, observed with pleasure the number of visible earthworms, and tipped the hair on top of them, and on top of all the banana skins, egg shells, and other unidentifiable muck.

The mantra with compost is that anything that has once lived can be composted, and made into the stuff of new life. Human hair is rich in nitrogen. Likewise human fingernail- and toe-clippings. There have been tests done in which crops dressed with human hair have outgrown and out-produced those given commercial slow-release fertilizers. There is a company in America that sells biodegradable mats made out of human hair. They are used to line the bottom of potted plants, or as mulch.

On the other hand, there was a hairdresser in England who got written up in the local papers because he was taking bags of his clients' hair home for use in his compost. The council intervened, and told him that he was misusing industrial waste. They forced him to take it to the tip instead.

One of my gardening books tells me that burying plugs of hair around the garden can also repel animals, such as rabbits and deer, that can devastate a rural garden. I doubt if it will have the same effect on the rats.

The problem is that hair takes a long time to break down, and I suspect that the thick wiry stuff that grows out of my son has a considerable half-life. After tipping out the bucket, I wondered if the great clod of dry body-trimmings would bother the worms and inhibit the microorganisms. I wondered if we should have chopped it finer, as I do with woody prunings.

I got the garden fork and began to mix the hair. It was rather like folding coconut into a chocolate cake. It took quite some time, and even when I was done I could see the odd strand and clump. I was halfway through the job when I realized how I must look. There, in the glow of the fluorescent lights of the carpark, I was behaving like a witch. I was stirring the cauldron. Hubble bubble.

But was burying my son's hair in the compost a bad idea? Or would the fact that his trimmings were becoming part of compost — the stuff of life — be good for him? I thought it should be the latter, but worried that it might be the former.

I went in, slightly anxious, to find my son hunched over the computer, somewhat diminished by being shorn, but looking otherwise fine and healthy.

He still doesn't know what happened to his hair. He must think, if he thinks about it at all, that I threw it into the landfill bin. In my mind, that would be far worse. Surely having parts with which one has a sympathetic connection buried in a modern landfill would be bad for the soul and the health?

But of course I am no witch. There are no witches. And surely compost, being the stuff of life, can only be good?

He is looking very well, my son. And his hair is growing again.

It tickles me to think that, in a season or two, he might be eating lettuce that contains some remainder of himself.

~

There is one secret of the professional gardeners that I would like to learn: How do you grow an iceberg lettuce that hearts properly?

My own preference is for a variety of loose-leaf lettuce — the kind that grows fast, comes in many different colors and textures, and can be harvested a few leaves at a time, solving the constant problem of the home gardener of dealing with gluts in available produce. In the pots that straddle my verandah railing, I have the soft, chewy leaves of Butterhead, the cunningly shaped Red Oak Leaf, a frilly variety called Red Salad Bowl, which puts me in mind of the kind of ornate tapestry cushions my grandmother used to like, and a variety I grow largely because of the name — 'Drunken Woman Frizzy-headed' — which has pale-green, crinkled leaves tinged with rose. Frankly, it tastes more boring than it looks, but no reader of seed catalogues could resist.

With all these, plus some rocket and raddichio, I can put together an interesting-looking salad with ease. The problem is that my children don't like these kinds of lettuce. They want iceberg or cos — lettuce that to my taste is insipid. They like it because it has a watery crunch. It offends me that when the garden is full of lettuce, my children still want me to buy them bland iceberg from the supermarket, so each year I try to grow it well enough to satisfy them, with the same kinds of neatly rolled heads of crisp, tasteless leaves. I have never succeeded, and because of the frequency of my failure, I take more than the usual care to follow to the letter the dictates of the scary gardening books.

They tell me that winter is the ideal time to grow this kind of lettuce. It doesn't like heat. The cool weather helps the heads to form. All one needs, supposedly, is fertile soil, ample sunlight, and cool weather.

Ample sunlight is always a challenge on the six square meters, but this autumn I resolved to devote some of my premium sunny space at the front of the house to the iceberg challenge. I started the seedlings in early autumn in little black pots by the back door, and set them out before the temperatures fell too far.

So far, so good. But two weeks ago, on my morning walk of the grounds, I found that my children are not the only ones who like iceberg. Surrounding the half-dozen plants were long gastropods — slugs. They really were quite beautiful. Encased in their coats of mucus, they were long, leathery, and dappled, as though they were wearing leopard-skin coats. I watched them for a while. I know it's weird, but I find slugs quite fascinating.

Take the way they get around. It is a wonder of evolution. It's extraordinary to think about all the different ways evolution has created for the simple business of locomotion. We have our legs and feet. Fish have fins, and the tight, muscular way they swim. Slugs have mucus and muscle. Put a slug on a sheet of glass, and you can see its foot contracting and relaxing in sequence, pushing and pulling it along.

Then there is sex. Slugs are hermaphrodites, with both male and female sex organs. Mating slugs exchange sperm through their corkscrew-shaped penises, and sometimes they get stuck. In which case, the slugs chew off each other's penises in order to get free. Their teeth, you see, are razor sharp, and this is useful for more than chewing iceberg lettuce. Once castrated, the slugs can mate only using their female organs.

Supposedly, there are many ways to deal with slugs, and over the years I have tried most of them. I have buried stale beer in smooth-sided glasses, in order to drown them. I have surrounded my tender seedlings with ash, and sawdust, and ground up eggshell, all of which in theory defeat their slimy means of getting around.

All of these methods have brought me only limited success. The best way of tacking slugs and snails is to tour the grounds in the early morning carrying a container of salt. Pick them up, and drop them in.

In the old days, when I had more than an acre of garden, I carried a bucket of salt. Today, it was enough to go back to the kitchen and put salt in an old yoghurt container. I returned to the slip of front garden, picked up the cold, wet creatures and dropped them in.

It is rather hard to maintain an idea of oneself as a kindly person when you are killing slugs in this way. The salt causes them to desiccate, drawing all the fluid out of their bodies — but it looks as though they are boiling. They writhe and wriggle, and the moisture runs gray into the salt. Once, I had chickens to which I could throw the residue. These days, the salty corpses go straight into the compost.

And so the iceberg lettuce seedlings were saved, and now they are close to harvest. However, I already know they will not satisfy my children. For some reason, they won't heart up. They are spread all spindly over the soil, the coarse outer leaves destined for discard, and the inner ones totally lacking the white crispness of acceptability. And I won't eat these lettuces either. They are dull things. Perhaps I should have left them for the slugs.

So how do the supermarkets do it? What is the trick to getting that furled, crisp head? Who will tell me the secret?

~

I am rather irritable at the moment. Perhaps it is the state of the world — the prospect of global warming, the knowledge that my children's lives are likely to be harder than mine have been. But I am blaming the daffodils.

The first of the season are sprouting on my pocket-handkerchief sundeck — bursts of yellow on sappy stems. It seems almost wrong for them to be so yellow and so confident of the coming of spring. It is still winter. They are early. I am quite annoyed with them, which is perverse.

As I have written earlier, I planted the bulbs very late in autumn, thanks to the endless round of general busyness that prevents me from getting on with the real stuff of life, such as my garden, in a timely manner. I remember digging in to the pots on the sundeck, using a trowel with a wonky handle, and muttering under my breath about Wordsworth.

I wandered lonely as a cloud
That floats on high o'er vales and hills,
When all at once I saw a crowd,
A host, of golden daffodils

Not much chance of loneliness around here, with the family shrubbery running riot through the place most evenings. I sometimes think I could do with a bit more loneliness. Then again, on those rare days when I have nothing to do, I find myself sitting and thinking — what next? And from there, it is a small step to 'is that all there is'? A bit of time in the garden can bring me to peace with myself, but it isn't working right now.

I remember it was raining, too, when I planted those daffodils, but I was determined to get the bulbs in. I was thinking of myself, weary from winter, a few months' hence.

I know from experience that in early spring the view from my loungeroom windows can be depressing. The compost bin is dormant. The silverbeet looks surly. There are no flowers, and in place of vales and hills, I have the view of the McDonald's drive-through with its host of golden arches. I wanted daffodils as well, to make me feel like a good gardener, a husbander of cheer.

Normally, my garden plans are made only in order to go astray. Things don't grow as I plan, or other things grow faster. But this plan worked. Daffodils are so bloody reliable. So now the pots on the sundeck are studded with strappy leaves, and stems topped with furled yellow buds, and, until I cut it a few minutes ago, there was this one arrogant or self-confident bloom ahead of all the rest, with its open-hearted, imprudent embrace of possibility.

'Hey, look at me,' it said, seemingly quite unaware of how easily it could be kicked from the ground, or shat upon by the pigeons, or gnawed by the rats. It was defying imperfection, and frailty. Damn it. Daffodils are uniform, and bright as paint. A fitting subject for an Andy Warhol painting; repeating and repeating and repeating. They have none of the quirkiness or individuality of trees, or roses, or parsnips.

Although there are different types (King Alfred, Hoop Petticoat, and so forth), within each variety they are alike, which is why we plant them in drifts and groups.

Let me describe this one, this pioneer.

The green of the stem is topped with a brown papery sheath, like a reverse dunce's cap. Then there is the yellow canopy of six petals, each with a shading of green at the base, and the tops slightly curly, like a newspaper just unrolled.

At the center of these petals is another round of yellow forming a cylinder with a serrated top, and inside the cylinder are the sexual parts of the daffodil, there for all to see — the furry stamen and pistil reaching up and out in the hope of gentle touch.

Daffy daffodils. They open themselves in this way to light and sun and rain, exposing their innards, advertising their vulnerability with a splash of color in the gray, shaded, pre-spring garden.

Spring is coming, the daffodils say. Hope springs eternal. And all that.

I am going to cut more of the furled yellow buds, put them in a vase, and watch them open in the warmth of my living room.

~

I have been filling out my tax return and meanwhile boiling up bones. The two activities go together, and are fitting for deep winter. There is an anxious feeling, to be sure, to realize that one's outgoings for the year have quite possibly exceeded one's income, a fact masked by revolving credit. But while the tax return is underway, the stock boils. Making stock, and taking stock. And, despite the worrying deficit, there is an anal satisfaction to tax time — the summing up of a year of life, and arriving at a neat series of figures. Meanwhile, the making of stock is a reassuring investment in domestic comfort, and thrift.

I bought big beef bones filled with marrow from the butcher's. I bought chicken necks, and giblets, and fish heads — great big bags of them. It cost me three dollars, all up. I took out of the freezer the plastic bag in which I store all the trimmings from meal preparation — carrot tops, onion skins, and odds and ends of vegetable and meat. Then I went out into my backyard and harvested everything flavorsome. I hunted under the weeds for the remains of the tarragon and the thyme, and tore sage leaves from the bush. I even found a spindly celery plant that was still trying to grow in the light-deprived back garden-bed. It was stringy beyond usefulness for salad, but the stockpot redeems all.

Making stock takes time, but as one of my favorite cooking books says: people who are too lazy or too busy to cook properly have to be stoics in order to tolerate the results. There is so much they have to put up with in the way of nasty, hasty meals, and artificial ingredients. Only stock makers and takers can afford to be delicate and fussy.

Stock, plus a store of pasta and rice, plus a vegetable garden, means that chicken noodle soup is only minutes away, and risotto always at hand. If you have stock, you can be comforted. You may have negative cash flow. You may not be able to remember your Australian Business Number. You may not have filled in your quarterly business activity statement. You may not understand GST. But you will not starve.

I made 12 liters of stock — five of beef, five of chicken, and two of fish. All made from scraps, and rubbish, and dark, earthbound vegetables. Cooled down, the stocks formed jellies. Now they are decanted into old milk cartons and stored in the freezer. The taxman might give me a small refund this year, in the unlikely event that my math is correct. We will be all right. The wolf may remain visible on a distant hilltop but, lock and stock, I have barred the door.

~

I have been dealing with the fruits of winter: to be specific, lemons. I have no room for a decent lemon tree — the gall-wasp infected specimen I keep in a pot graces us with only half a dozen fruit a year, despite doses of potash and muttered threats, but a good friend of mine is moving house, and the tree in the backyard is laden with fruit, some the size of grapefruit. I have been taking the opportunity to harvest as many as I can before I lose access. Yesterday, I took the shopping trolley round and loaded it up. Now my fridge and my three fruit bowls are full, and the whole house smells of citrus. The family thinks I am mad. Why take more than you can use? Perhaps I am greedy. I love the bounty, the getting of lots of stuff for free, and my head is full of thoughts of lemons.

I can use them. I have made three tubs of lemon curd. Tonight, we will have lemon meringue pie. I have squeezed lemon juice over potatoes and baked them in the oven. I have squeezed another dozen or so, and frozen the juice in ice-cube trays to grace gin and tonics in the summer months to come.

I found a recipe for preserved lemons that seems deceptive in its simplicity. Cut the lemons in quarters, freeze overnight, thaw, pack with salt and bay leaves and peppercorns, and cover with more lemon juice. Then let it steep, and use the peel in summer pastas and tagines. In this way, we will carry winter into summer.

Two themes suggest themselves as I do this work — the power of human urine, and the power of the passage of time.

The first theme arises because of another lemon tree in another city, many years ago, in the back garden of a shared house. Once, it was a weak and spindly thing. Unbeknown to the owners of the house, one of their tenants (I will call him Hugh, which is not his real name) took to having a regular morning urination on the soil beneath its leaves.

He confided his habit to me after reading a few examples of my gardening writing. He obviously thought I was the sort of person who would understand, and possibly approve. He swore me to secrecy, which meant that every time I visited this shared house I took great pleasure in commenting at length on the vigor of the lemon tree, and watching him blush while the owners of the house accepted my praise.

Soon everyone was remarking on the lemon tree's extraordinary turn-around. It bore fruit of extraordinary quantity and quality. There was homemade lemonade. There was lemon to be eaten with fish. There were lemons to be given away.

Life is very long. So much happens to us between the beginning and the end.

Hugh found true love, and left the share house. He married. They were desperate for children, but at first it seemed as though they must be cursed. One child was stillborn. Two more miscarried. The people who used to share that house and I met at the funerals and memorial services for those children, who had been so present in their parents' plans and thoughts, and yet had never lived in the sunlit world. It is extraordinary what human beings can put up with, and survive. There was no bottom to the parents' grief. Yet they went on.

I remember visiting the mother in hospital during her fourth pregnancy. Given her history, she had been brought into what used to be called confinement, midway through the pregnancy, and was confined to bed. Without any assistance from the artificial fertility industry, and at a time when she surely would have embraced a complete lack of complications, she was carrying twins.

This time, they were born safely, and thrived.

It's strange to think that we tend to cohere at times of joy and sadness. I saw this couple after the birth. I was there when the twins turned one. And then life got busy, and I fell out of touch.

Through all this time, the lemon tree continued to grow. I visited this house a few times a year, and in winter was often given bags of fruit. Yes, it seemed to have lost some of its magical vigor now that it no longer had the benefits of daily urine, but it had turned the corner. It was strong. It continued, and gave fruit. I kept Hugh's secret. I did not tell the owners of this house about the urination.

It was almost exactly three years ago that I took a phone call from the owner of this house. I remember distinctly that I was walking to work. He had bad news.

Hugh was dead. He had killed himself — hung from a beam in the garden shed.

The brain freezes, receiving news of that sort. For hours I did not know what to think. Somewhere I sensed a great hole opening in my understanding of the world. And around the rim of this hole, in this ugly, barely acknowledged image in my mind, all the people I know, myself included, were crawling, trying to carry on despite the revelation of the maw beneath.

There was another funeral.

It took some months for that hole in my mind to close, or recede, or whatever the right word is for a dreadful thing that somehow you manage to stop thinking about.

The twins grew up. Life went on. And sometime in the grieving period I told my friends about the urination on their lemon tree.

As I pack another crop of lemons in salt, there is another not unrelated theme that comes to me. It is the passing of time, and the healing effects of this.

The children's father and I separated many years ago, during the days when I had my big garden, and another sickly lemon tree. We remained on reasonable terms, and I was able to ask him to attempt to revive my lemon tree with a daily urination. I will spare you the details of the request and the performance, but once again it worked. The lemon tree became vigorous and prolific.

I remember an afternoon from that time when the children decided they wanted to visit their father without escort. He lived just up the hill, in a house we had organized so we could continue to co-parent. This would be the longest journey — some 300 meters — they would have attempted on their own. I decided to let them. There was little that could hurt them out there — very few cars to speak of, and fewer people, and if I stood in the road I could see them almost all the way to their father's door.

They held hands because I had told them to look after each other. Off they went, up the hill into the afternoon light, four and three years old, full of their own daring and grown-upness. When they got near the top they turned and waved, and I heard my daughter say to her little brother 'look how far we've come'. Then they disappeared, and, of course, arrived at their father's safe and proud.

It is years, now, since I contacted Hugh's widow and the twins. Too long. I will correct this before spring.

~

The weather has been perfect here in Melbourne; the very best of crisp, blue winter. Meanwhile, I have spent most of the week shut in my office at the university, looking out at a courtyard festooned with bicycles, trying to convince myself that writing the latest grant application is meaningful work, when all I really want to do is perform the work I am talking about, rather than persuading someone else they should give me money to do it.

So often, the thing we really need is time. This is true of almost everything we do. But these days, thinking, reading, and writing is graced, in the academic world, with the grand word 'research' — once reserved for the sciences and other fields of empirical inquiry. Research means research funding, and that means grant applications. So budgets must be constructed, and timelines determined. We must apply for research assistants, when we know that managing them will take almost as much time as they save. Without research grants, we are reminded, the whole enterprise of the university wobbles and may founder.

There is nothing like working in an office for a while to make you realize what a luxury it is to work from home. Freedom, though, brings with it insecurity. It is a trade I have been willing to make for most of my life, but now I work at the university, and they pay me the same in a productive week as in an unproductive one, and a completed grant application counts as productivity.

All this is nobody's fault, or nobody within the reach of my influence. Universities are funded largely on their success in achieving research outcomes and gaining grants, and in this dance the humanities must participate the same as anyone else. Nor is it pointless. Some research does require travel, transcription of interviews, public opinion surveys, the doing of things so that their impact can be studied. All this takes money, and universities have only small pots available, and these are awarded with a stipulation that the work must lead to a research-grant application. We write more grant applications than journal articles or books, I think. It has become core academic work, putting out the begging bowl.

So I sat there drinking too much coffee, and in between writing paragraphs pulled from thin air, yet phrased in an attempt to sound entirely convinced and convincing, I realized I had been overwatering the solitary cactus that is my only office-bound plant. There was something about the grant application writing process, the constructing of theoretical frameworks to justify my curiosity, that had made me over-attentive to this virtually self-sufficient succulent. It is planted in a teapot. I bought it one week when I was being attacked in the pages of the national daily. I thought that the presence of a growing thing in a teapot would give me a kind of double-barrelled comfort and necessary perspective.

It had worked, and yet now the writing of my learned begging letter had unhinged my understanding of what care was needed. Every time I went to get a coffee, I had also been fetching water for the cactus, and now it was awash.

I don't even like cactus, I muttered to myself. I looked at it crossly. I was getting increasingly homesick for my backyard and its growing things, and for my former life as a freelance journalist, able to sally forth and ask questions about almost anything, providing I could persuade some editor somewhere that they might like to publish an article about it.

On the day I lodged the grant application, after many late nights, I rang a colleague and inveigled him into a brief escape. We went to the zoo — an easy walk away. My friend is a philosopher with a speciality in ethics. He harbors a deep identification with bears. Having paid those creatures an obligatory visit, we watched the sleek antics of the otters and the meditative munching of the gorillas, and then went for an ice-cream. We were commenting on the quality of Melbourne's zoo compared to others we have known. He said of one zoo 'I have never seen so many neurotic animals.' After a pause he added: 'Except at the university.'

The next day, cycling to work and feeling myself chafe at the necessities of academic life, I decided to divert to check out whether one of my personal Melbourne reference points remained as I remember it. Winter is the best time for this, and I had not yet made a visit during the season.

I am referring to a particular gum tree in the Carlton Gardens. You can see it best while sitting in your car or on your bike, facing east, at the junction of Queensberry and Rathdowne streets. It is a supremely graceful tree, with art nouveau curves, and polished gray-white bark. It seems to glow against the European foliage that surrounds it. When I used to drive this way more frequently, I looked forward to seeing this tree. It seemed to me very special — always beautiful, yet always changing with the seasons.

I huffed my way up Queensberry Street, riding past the trendy

French patisserie, the boutique shops, the many places that depend on people like me having money to spend, and therefore regular jobs. I also passed the red-brick building on Queensberry Street that houses some part of the University that I know nothing about — some school or department doubtless full of good people and rigorous inquiry, yet closed to the work of my department, and my inquiries, even though we are only a block away. After all, none of us have the time for each other.

But at last I was facing the gardens, and there it was, at its best against the winter sky, its branches sinuous, its bark silvery and many-colored like mother-of pearl, its leaves a dancing mop against the sky. It had changed, of course. Trees grow, whether or not we are there to observe them doing so. Yet it was also the same.

I went to work and gave a lecture, and somewhere in the middle of it I sensed that something had happened. I had managed to teach something. A young man, as lost as any scholar can be, was gazing at me with his mouth partly open. He shook himself, and began to type frantic notes. Our eyes met.

I went back to my office feeling privileged, fetched my cactus teapot, and poured the excess liquid down the faculty sink.

—

The gardening books will tell you that a vegetable patch should be placed so as to get eight hours of direct sunlight each day. This, like so much advice in gardening books, is a counsel of perfection. If I took it to heart, I would have no garden at all. Only the narrow strip of soil in my front yard gets anything like eight hours. In the years since I started to try to grow things in my six square meters, I have gained a lot of knowledge about what will grow in less than eight hours of sunlight, and what will not. Most of my space is behind the house, shaded by the trees in the McDonald's carpark and by the laughable so-called privacy screen that in theory prevents me from peering at my neighbors. This privacy was a requirement of the building inspector when we extended the house. It is entirely ineffective. Because it is perforated, I could, if I wished, observe my neighbor's every move, if she ever went into the back garden, which she does not. These are the flimsy means by which we inner-suburbanites try to pretend that we don't live on top of each other, that we retain some autonomy, agency, and independence.

However, the privacy screen does cast most of my garden in shade. I have two raised garden-beds. One sits immediately in front of the privacy screen, and is in total shade. The other is on the opposite side of the yard, and gains shafts of light in the morning and the afternoon.

The patch in total shade is my biggest challenge. Here I have planted a Kaffir lime, which is grown for its fragrant leaves rather than its golf-ball sized, corrugated-skinned fruits, which are unbearably bitter. The leaves can be mashed into curry paste, or added to salad. The lime tree has grown tall, above the privacy screen, seeking every bit of light. I have enough lime leaves to supply a dozen restaurants, and I regularly prune it back and place the cut branches at the front of the house, free to a good home.

Next to this tree, squeezed between compost bin and fence

but with the potential ability to reach the shaft of light that makes its way down the back lane, I have planted a mandarin that has never fruited, despite also growing tall to reach the sun. Given my limited space, I shouldn't tolerate its lack of productivity. I should rip it out and devote the space to something else, but each year so far I have fertilized, pruned, and (on the advice of one of my wackier gardening books) muttered threats. This year, it carried three perfect white blossoms. All of them failed to form into fruit. I have plans for a fig tree, if I can summon up the ruthlessness to kill the mandarin.

I am always hopeful that I will be able to break the rules of gardening, and I have attempted to grow things — both fruit and flower — in front of these trees. I was told that comfrey would grow anywhere, and become a weed and a ground cover. I am here to tell you that this is wrong. The comfrey died. Sorrel is meant to grow in wet, damp, dark, boggy spots. Not for me, or not in this space.

The only thing that has survived and thrived are canna lilies, which each spring reward me. They have even grown under the spiral staircase that leads from the verandah to the brick paving. They seem quite indestructible, which is perhaps why these perfect white trumpets and their erect, waxy yellow pistils are so often associated with funerals. They speak, not of death, but of the persistence of life.

Across the way, in the garden bed that has a little more sun, I have found that dark, leafy vegetables seem to do well. Chard and silverbeet are the hero vegetables of partial shade. The lack of light seems to encourage the growth of big, thick leaves — fleshier than normal, and spread wide like umbrellas to catch as much sun as possible. Perhaps because life is tough, they also seem to produce for a longer season. Shaded silverbeet is slower to go to seed. Amaranth also produces a worthwhile crop in partial shade, but runs quickly to seed, becoming so leggy, and full of stem and scanty leaves, that it is hardly worth the trouble of the harvest, or the space it takes up.

Parsley also responds to reduced daylight, particularly if you allow it to self-seed, but coriander is much fussier. Don't bother unless you can provide it with the requisite eight hours. Lemon balm can manage in shade, but looks sullen, and succumbs readily to thrips.

Strawberries, one gardening book told me, are a forest-floor fruit, and can therefore cope with dappled light. It isn't true, in my experience, or else there must be more dapples in the forest than in my backyard, because the strawberries planted in partial shade never fruit, and die at the first sign of adversity.

A rule of thumb is that if you grow a plant for the fruit or the root, it needs full sun. If you grow it for the leaves, stems or buds, then at least some shade will be tolerated. This rule is a good general guide. There is no point growing beans, or peas, or tomatoes, or eggplant in less than full sun. All those plants are relegated to the front yard and my precious few meters of full-sun garden-bed. Nevertheless, there are exceptions to the rule.

This year, I experimented with a couple of berry varieties that claimed to be able to grow in half-light. The tayberry is a cross between a raspberry and a blackberry. I planted it in the only space I had left — a makeshift garden-bed half obscured behind a timber seat. It sat and did nothing for a year, but with the end of winter it has taken off, and is climbing the back fence, reaching for the light. So far there have been none of the promised aromatic, cone-shaped fruits, but I am encouraged by the vigor of the plant to hope for good results by summer.

As for the rest of my shaded backyard, I still search the garden nurseries each spring in hope of finding miracle shade-tolerant plants, and more exceptions to the rules. I am always condemning sun-lovers to an early death by planting them in the hope they will prove the gardening books wrong.

Perhaps because I am demanding perverse behavior, sometimes things become very weird indeed. I have one miracle silverbeet plant that has been producing for more than two years now, although silverbeet is meant to be an annual. Its stem has become a giant, gnarled thing, like a portion of tree root lying horizontally on the soil. Leaves sprout for its entire length, some of them forming independent root systems and becoming plants in their own right — meaning that it is now many seasons since I have planted silverbeet seed. This single plant and its progeny have become my reliable vegetable, refusing to die, and always producing greenery when the rest of the garden is bare, and the vegetable crisper empty. We could eat silverbeet every day of the week if we wished, and the triffid would simply grow more. Perhaps one day it will die, but at the moment it seems more likely to take over the patch. I think I have bred a mutant out of my adversity.

SPRING

Things are going to seed. I don't mean in a bad way. There are none of the musty smells and nasty stains that we imagine when we talk of people and buildings that are past their best. Instead, the warming weather has sent all those things that grow slowly through winter, providing me with edible flowerheads and plentiful leaves, into their seasonal rush to propagate. There are yellow broccoli flowers bobbing in my front garden, the rocket has grown higher than the balcony balustrade, and the cos lettuce have taken on the look of green-shelled rockets, their central tubes of leaves pushing higher every day. The flower heads will pop out any hour now, the tight roll of leaves will collapse and grow bitter, and it will all be over for those plants this season. It is time for the hurried making of salads, and for planting new seedlings before the year tips over into heat.

Thank God for sheet mulching, I tell myself. Cover up all the weeds with the newspapers presently stacked on the front verandah, add heaps of blood and bone and straw, and I know that I will be able to transform the garden very quickly — when I get the time. But I have recently stopped subscribing to newspapers in hard copy. I read them on my iPad instead. I think a whole tradition of permaculture is about to die if everyone does the same. The permaculture movement rests largely on the assumption that everyone has lots of newspaper for sheet mulching.

It already seems warm enough to plant beans and peas. One of my gardening books advises that the way to judge this is by sitting bare-buttocked on the ground. If your bum doesn't get cold, it is time to plant. Given that my back verandah is visible from the McDonald's drive through, and the little strip of land at the front faces the post office, I won't be trying this method. An index finger in the soil will have to do.

Am I imagining that the seasons are coming faster now? Usually, it is October before I lose the winter brassicas to flower. Normally gardening relaxes me, but the possibility that the seasons are altering their archetypal pattern — that the climate change we all fear is already upon us — means that my trips into the garden are tinged with anxiety. Not already, surely. Not here, in my garden. Please.

I often think about Voltaire, who, contemplating the broken nature of the world and our powerlessness in putting it to rights, declared that 'we must cultivate our garden'. But Voltaire lived at a time when nobody imagined the possibility that human beings would change the climate. For him, and for the generations that preceded him, the seasons were a fixed certainty, the basis of religious metaphor, story, and myth. If we are changing our climate, we are changing the schema of our world. We are changing a part of what it means to be human. And standing here, on my little patch of inner-suburban earth, I feel very frightened.

I have cut the broccoli flowers and put them in a vase, and I will use a shovel to hack the remainder of the plants into compost-friendly sections, making the soil bare for new plantings and new experiments in life and death.

~

There is some controversy in the gardening world about whether one can re-use potting mix. My own position is torn between thriftiness and the desire for certainty of outcome, which of course cannot be achieved either in the garden or in life. I want my plants to grow, and potting mix that has already yielded a crop must surely be exhausted. Yet driving to the garden center and paying too much good money for dirt goes against the grain. It offends both my sense of sustainability and my purse.

I am forced to use a lot of pots because I have only a small space, and an even smaller space that gets sufficient daylight to grow what I want to grow. If I bought new potting mix every season, it would cost me hundreds of dollars, and help to exhaust the peat moss bogs, the vermiculite mines, and the sources of coconut fiber, as well as all the other businesses in the world that gather, pack, and ship the raw material for the potting mixes. Thousands of human beings, hundreds of different landscapes, vast logistical operations involving trucks and ships and human labor, all so I can grow a lettuce in the Melbourne sun. There must be a better way.

It is possible to make your own potting mix. Screen your compost, the gardening blogs advise, then pasteurize it by putting it in the oven. This can then be mixed with rotted sawdust gathered from your friendly neighborhood sawmill, and soil.

The problem, of course, is the practicality of this. I have no room to store sawdust, nor do I have a friendly neighborhood sawmill. I have only Bunnings, who bag and sell their sawdust to the makers of commercial composts (I asked). If I were to attempt to bake sufficient sieved compost to fill my pots, the oven would be going flat out for days. Lastly, even a compost enthusiast like me lacks the time and will to strain my compost, ridding it of the avocado skins and seeds, the sweetcorn husks and the worms.

So I compromise, and try to re-use my potting mix for as long as possible. Each season, I pull out the plants from their pots, shaking the dirt off the rootballs. Sometimes there is nothing BUT rootball — great masses of plant matter like old lady's hair, all thin and wiry and set hard. Then the whole thing goes in to the top of the compost bin, because there is no distinction between the growing medium and the thing that has grown — a strangely awe-inspiring state of affairs, testament at once to the limits of container growing, and to the power inherent in every tiny seed.

Having got rid of the rootballs, I tip the remaining old potting mix into a big heap in the middle of the backyard. I undo the ratcheting straps that hold my sagging compost bin together, and dig out as much of the stuff as seems reasonably digested, trying to leave behind the still-decomposing bits, and find and discard all the other odd things that one finds in home-made compost:

the vegetable knife I lost six months ago, the bits of Lego, and — perennial mystery — a leg from a Barbie doll.

While I do this, all the life of the pots and the compost heap attempts to escape, and some of it tries to bite me. There are the redback spiders that have over-wintered in the pots and the heap. Centipedes flow like water over the semi-digested bits of eggshell. Worms, suddenly exposed to light and predators, do whatever they can to regain the dark. They burrow between the brick pavers and hide in squirmy bunches under the shovel. I scoop them all in to the mix, thinking that this must be good — a *real* soil, such as one might find on a forest floor. Nothing is too neat. Everything is messy with life and death.

I pick out the Lego and the lost vegetable knives, but each year I mix in the Barbie leg, knowing I will find it again next spring when I redo the pots. It will be festooned with roots. It will be part of a rootball. Thus it will find its way back into the compost bin for a round of the seasons, then back into the pots, then round again. There is something in me — I hesitate to call it feminism — that takes pleasure in this part of a doll, some people's idea of perfect womanhood, mixed with dirt, and worms, and the real stuff of fertility.

Using my shovel like a giant spoon, I mix the compost with the potting mix, and sprinkle blood and bone like icing sugar over a cake. I refill all the pots with the mixture. Anything left over goes in the top of the compost bin, with the theory being that a few hundred buckets of kitchen scraps will in time refresh it.

Does this work? Who knows. Sometimes things grow.

Sometimes they don't. When they don't grow, I wonder about my method. When they do, I assume that it is simply the universe on my side. Surely there must be a limit to this zero-sum game — a point beyond which one cannot cheat the commercial gods of gardening. At some stage, the potting mix must cease to work. If I were a different kind of person, I would conduct a proper experiment: lettuces in old potting mix, and lettuces in new, to see if it makes a difference. One day, I will do just that. Then I will have knowledge on which I will be forced to act. But for the moment, I mix my mud puddings, think of Barbie under the lettuce seedlings with the worms, and prefer not to know.

~

The persistent miracle of gardening, and parenthood for that matter, is that things grow despite one's incompetence.

When I was newly pregnant with my first child, I remember looking through the early spring crop of seed catalogues with fear in my heart. After all, so many seeds fail to grow. Some rot. Some push out tender green shoots, and the snails finish them off. It seemed improbable to me that any should grow at all, and therefore unlikely that the cluster of cells inside me should grow to a healthy child.

Now spring has come around for the nineteenth time since those frightened reflections, and the child I couldn't quite believe in will shortly leave home. Once again, I am looking through the old shoe box in which I keep my seeds to see what I need to order, and to try and work out a way of finding space for all the things I want to grow. There is so much variety. The sand-like black seeds of poppies, the miniature burrs of carrot, the smooth, hard broad beans. The broad-bean seed is just the right size, I remember, for toddlers to put up their nostrils. When my son was a toddler, we had a hurried trip to casualty because of a bean stuck in the nose. 'How did it get in there?' I asked him. 'I opened my nose and a bean fell in,' he replied.

I remember a few years later trying to explain to him how he was made, and came to grow in my tummy.

'Daddy planted a seed …'

Now my son is over six feet tall. He rests his chin on the top of my head as a sign of affection. He has entered the grunty, apparently pre-verbal stage of late adolescence. His involvement in the garden is limited to helping me move and lift things, and only then under sufferance.

The children are all grown. They tell me they want to be left alone, and not to nag. They find out my deepest principles — principles I didn't even know that I had — and flout them. So much planning and care, and then growing things trip you up and make you a fool.

Things grow according to their nature. You can train and trellis, but plants still struggle to be themselves. It's one of the things that make gardening fascinating. But sometimes, you get to cheat.

Last year, I discovered my local garden center has cunning, and distressingly expensive, pots designed to straddle a balcony railing. I requested one for my birthday present, which caused the teenagers to roll their eyes, but they bought it nevertheless and I was a convert. Now I have six of these pots balanced on my little sundeck balustrade, growing bok choy, strawberries, radishes, and lettuce.

Even more novel are the upside-down bags, bought for two dollars each on special from Bunnings. I assumed at the time that they were cheap because they didn't work, and nobody else was foolish enough to purchase. There isn't much to them. The bags are like green sausages, around a meter long, with a little hole at the bottom and a big one at the top, together with some wires, and a hook by which to hang them.

The idea is that you push a seedling's leaves through the bottom hole, leaving the roots in the bag, fill from the top with potting mix, water it, and hang it in a sunny spot so the plant grows upside down. I have planted an eggplant, a tomato, and a capsicum, and hung the bags from the only part of my sundeck railing not occupied by the straddling pots. They look like fat, premature Christmas stockings.

The picture on the package showed tomato plants growing like upside-down trees, trailing below the bag and laden with fruit, but my plants are behaving differently. They clearly want to grow up. Just after their stems emerge from the bag, they take a U-turn and are struggling upwards against gravity. How will they fare once they (hopefully) set fruit? Will they be able to continue the upward thrust, or will they snap off and die? There is a ghastly fascination to watching this play out.

~

I always have to restrain myself at this time of year. A few days of sunshine, and blossoms popping, and magpies swooping at my head when I walk the dog in the park, and I want to plant out the zucchini and pumpkin seedlings.

I must hold off. Previous years have made me think the weather bureau should employ me as a reliable predictor of the last frost of the season. It always comes three days after I plant out my tender seedlings. At the moment, I am having particular trouble holding myself back from the garden. This is because I am writing a book, and also because it is spring. The tasks I have put off all year suddenly seem very urgent indeed, but when I am writing, cleaning out the linen cupboard seems urgent, as does tidying my sock drawer. When I am mid-project, writing is misery. Every day brings a miasma of doubt and frustration. People assume that because I have written previous books, I know how it is done. It isn't true. I know, sort of, how I did those previous books. I don't know how to do the present one. Writing is a constant battle with feelings of incompetence. My theme tune, mid project, is T.S. Eliot's poem 'The Hollow Men'.

Shape without form, shade without color,
Paralysed force, gesture without motion;

And, later in the same poem:

Between the conception
And the creation
Between the emotion
And the response
Falls the Shadow

In this horrible shadowland, the garden keeps me sane. I plant seedlings — far too many. I want to plant out those zucchini so I can bank on a surplus, an embarrassment of swollen, green fruit. Then I can give them away to my neighbors, the product of my labor. Surely that will be enough. It ought to be enough. What perversity to feel it necessary to also write a book.

Yesterday was a good day. I allowed myself to procrastinate, and garden. My brain went on holiday, and the rest of me went on all fours as I weeded and planted out so many lettuce seedlings that it is hard to believe we will eat anything else this summer.

There is something meditative about being so close to the soil. My thoughts meander in odd ways, making strange connections. Sometimes I feel as though I am having a conversation with an older, wiser part of myself. Sometimes I wonder if this is what it is like to pray. The only other times this happens to me are when I am falling asleep, or when I am on a long car journey. Always, it is something to do with letting go and focusing simultaneously. First, I think about television programs I have seen, books I have read, conversations I have had. Then all that drifts away and I am in the moment, barely thinking at all. Who needs a mantra, when weeds are all pervasive?

And so I found myself liberated from the book, and instead reflecting on soil structure, and the different methods of tenacity displayed by the weeds. One weed — I think it is called a marshmallow plant — has tough brown roots that go deep, meaning one pulls up half the garden bed in getting it out. Dandelions, too, have deep taproots reaching far down beyond the reach of my trowel. But there are other weeds so shallow-rooted that one wonders why they bother. All one has to do is brush the soil, and they are lying there unrooted, their filaments drying in the sun.

Clumps of grass take such a firm hold that it is disheartening. They seem convinced that they belong. I often guiltily remember a gardening book I once read that said, rather fiercely, 'Grass has no place in the vegetable garden.' All my vegetable gardens since then have seemed determined to disprove this statement.

Then later, planting out all those lettuces, I reflected on the arrogance of use-by dates when it comes to a miracle like a seed. You see, the reason I have so many lettuce seedlings is that the seed I used was all out of date, so I sowed it thickly, expecting only a little to come up.

Virtually every seed germinated, meaning that I had boxes and boxes of crowded seedlings, their leaves struggling for light and their lower parts white and spindly, like legs on the beach on the first day of summer. I have planted many varieties. The names are very pleasing. Buttercrunch, Sucrine, Cos, Oakleaf, Radicchio, and Iceberg. They sound like liquors, or sweets, or the capitals of foreign nations.

Crawling inch by inch over the earth planting them out, my mind wandered, and I saw minutely the way the individual grains of sandy soil were bound together with roots alive and dead. I counted the earthworms. I got muck under my fingernails. And, as it always does in the garden, happiness crept up on me. There are times when I think I would be happy to be a gardener, and nothing else. Why is it after all, that we feel the need to be more, or different?

And this morning, as I plucked up the courage to climb the stairs to my study, and switch on the computer, there was T.S. Eliot again.

There will be time, there will be time
To prepare a face to meet the faces that you meet.

~

The word 'brassica' has always filled me with deep ambivalence.

It comes, according to my dictionary, from the Latin word for cabbage, but in English it refers to a whole family of traditionally uninspiring vegetables including brussels sprouts, cabbage, broccoli, and turnips.

Brassica sounds so exotic, so rococo. Cabbage, turnip, and brussels sprout sound so English, and so boring. The smell of cabbage cooking is a cliché in novels. It stands for depression, poverty, and dreariness. In *1984*, George Orwell wrote of dreary buildings that always smelled of boiled cabbage. No one who cooks cabbage could possibly make pesto. Or at least, not in the world of fiction.

And yet, in midwinter in this part of the world, brassicas are often the only fresh greens available, and if, like me, you regard it as a personal failure to have to buy a vegetable, then that means that you try to focus on the wonderful sound of brassica, and forget the soggy associations of cabbage.

Why, though, am I thinking of brassicas now, when the sweet new peas are springing out of the ground, and fresh beans are only a week or two away? It is because of this rather wonderful plant that I discovered more or less by accident, called perennial broccoli.

Just when all the other brassicas are behind me, this huge plant that has taken up space at the back of the vegetable patch all winter has me awestruck. Unlike most broccoli, this is not a fussy plant. Most broccoli is hardly worth the trouble. It must be protected from cabbage whites, gives you a fine flurry of dark-green heads through summer, must be cut every day if it is not to go to seed, then finally, when you neglect it for just one day, goes all leggy and precious, sprouts yellow flowers, then dies on you.

But the perennial broccoli has survived over winter, getting bigger and bigger, taking over its corner, and shrugging off the attentions of the cabbage whites. I found myself getting impatient with it over winter, because it sagged, sulked, and sheltered whole colonies of snails. 'Cabbage,' I thought resentfully.

But now there are tiny cauliflower-like heads, cream-colored with a touch of purple, that steam beautifully, and are so pungent they are almost hot. 'Brassica, brassica,' I whisper under my breath as I harvest. Truly, this is a vegetable deserving of a Latin name.

~

Homesickness can take you by surprise, and right in the midst of the thrill of travel. I am presently in Shanghai, a city that feels like the center of the world. Manhattan used to feel this way. I imagine London felt like this at the time Samuel Johnson asserted that if a man was tired of London, then he was tired of life.

Shanghai is such an exciting place. Last night I walked along the Bund, with colonial buildings on one side of the river, and the extravagant present of the Pudong skyscrapers on the other. There is nowhere like this in the world. This is a city caught in the act of destruction and creation. Only a generation ago, there was starvation in this country. The parents of the people who crowd the food courts and the shopping malls can remember people eating grass to fill their stomachs. China is a miracle, and I am lucky to be here.

And yet. There was a moment yesterday, as I sat on a bus travelling through the frayed outer suburbs of the city, when I wished to be at home, pottering in my few square meters of soil. From the bus, I could see old men carrying plastic buckets of water on poles as they tended their perfectly square vegetable plots. All around their remnant farms were factories, and twenty-storey apartment blocks, and building sites. These market gardens will, no doubt about it, have been built over by this time next year.

Further out, there were fields of rice. Every little farmhouse had a pond crowded with ducks. Every space was used to grow something. The men worked the fields with hoes and rakes, and scattered what looked like fertilizer by hand, out of a bucket. They were all old men. China has now had two decades of the one-child policy. Most of those children will gravitate to the city, carrying solo the hopes and expectations of their parents, and two sets of grandparents.

Meanwhile, the air was like soup. The pollution in China literally takes your breath away, and makes your eyeballs sting. If you have ever doubted that it is possible for human beings to so damage their environment that it becomes poison, then come to China.

The papers are reporting that children are being diagnosed with lung cancer — a disease that normally takes decades to develop — as young as seven.

Sitting high up on the highway, viewing the farmers from my bus, knowing that they will soon be built over, or relocated, or simply unable to continue, I felt a longing to tend my own little patch. I was wondering if the passionfruit vine had grown to the top of the trellis.

I was thinking of my little sundeck, my tomato plant and eggplant growing upside down in their suspended grow-bags, and the lettuce that was just coming into its own. I was wondering whether anyone at home had thought to water the plants. My stomach clenched with homesickness.

At that moment, I thought how fine it is to have a home, to

understand its customs and its ways, and to plant a seed and watch it grow, knowing that (if it is not tempting fate to think so) life will be much the same next year as it is this.

China is a miracle, and a dilemma. It doesn't have that luxury.

~

George Bernard Shaw, whom I have quoted earlier in these reflections, once said that the only unquestionably useful activity was gardening. It is not a statement that can be made with the same degree of confidence on this side of the world. We have cultivated monsters, such as blackberry thickets and plagues of rabbits, in our attempt to prove we control the natural world.

In spite of all the things Europeans have planted on this continent that we now wish we hadn't, the urge to cultivate continues, even when most of us live such urban lives that we feel more need to create havens from the urban wilderness than make statements about our relationship to the natural world.

How does this work in the inner city? I regard the McDonald's carpark at the rear of my house as a kind of wilderness. The post office opposite my house at the front is, on the other hand, an example of the nice things we mean when we claim to be civilized. All the people of the world come there.

My suburb is divided between people like me, with nice houses, and the other half, those who live in high-rise housing commission flats. We hardly ever meet, except in the queue for service at the post office. Alongside them is the local solicitor, the grocer banking change, the schoolchild buying stationery, and me after a postage stamp — all of us served according to our place in the queue with the measured, sustainable patience of people who spend their whole day on their feet in service.

But I digress. I have been trying to contain the spring growth on a budget. Money is tight, but things are growing all over the place. This is not a how-to book, as I have said, but I find to my satisfaction that I have come up with some good solutions to satisfy the civilizing urge on a budget. So here are some hints for organizing your wilderness on the cheap.

If you go to a gardening shop, you will pay top dollar for treated pine trellis, but there is a cheaper and easier way. Buy weld mesh, of the type used for reinforcing concrete. It is amazingly cheap. Hammer some star pickets into the ground, and use fencing wire to attach the mesh to the pickets. Result — instant trellis. It doesn't look as good as the treated pine stuff from the gardening shop, but that will only matter until the plants grow to cover it.

Proper gardeners spend a lot of time constructing gravel paths. I don't have the time, so recently I adapted the sheet-mulching method of gardening to the making of a path. I laid newspaper over short-cut grass to kill it, and then simply spread the gravel over the top. A few rain showers later, and the whole thing had settled enough to make quite an acceptable walking surface.

If you have no money for pots, go to the fruit and vegetable market and ask for some of the sturdy polystyrene boxes in which they pack broccoli and the like. Normally, they will give them to you for free, or at most ask for a few cents in return. Punch holes in the bottom, fill with potting mix and compost, and plant away. One deep box is usually enough to support a cucumber vine, or three lettuce, or an unlimited crop of cut-and-come-again cress.

That's it. No more hints.

~

I am alarmed to find everyone asking me the names of plants, how tall I think certain things will grow, and even apologizing for the quality of their compost heaps. It seems people think that if you write about gardening, you must be an expert. Nothing could be further from the truth. Enthusiast, yes. Expert, no. My own garden resembles a rubbish tip, with small examples of grace and functionality amid the mess.

But sometimes I can be useful. There was a message on my answering machine earlier this week from a friend. 'What do I do about snails?' she said. I was wondering myself. In spite of El Niño, and the dire predictions of no rain to speak of until winter, we had just come through a very soggy few days, and the snails that had disappeared for weeks were out, and ravenous.

As a child, I could quite happily spend hours playing with a snail, and I was upset when my mother crushed them. I also collected caterpillars in jars, and grew experimental mould factories on old oranges kept at the back of my wardrobe. Apart from this, to my mother's frustration, I showed no interest in gardening.

I would touch the feelers of my pet snails, and watch how they would instantly fold back in on themselves, like socks being turned inside out, and disappear. I still find that extraordinary. Where do they go? Into the brain space? Do snails have brains and, if so, what do they think about?

But none of this solves the problem of how to get rid of snails when you don't want them. Here is the sum total of my knowledge on the problem, followed by what I actually do. You can bury jam jars filled with old beer, or sugar and water, in the garden. In theory, the snails come to feed, fall in, and can't get out.

You can put hollowed-out grapefruit and orange skins between your plants. In theory, the snails crawl in for shelter during the day, making them easy to collect and destroy.

You can buy a duck. This one really works. Ducks love to eat snails, but ducks need water, and other ducks for company, and they have very unpleasant watery shit. They are not an option for the inner suburbs.

You can put circles of ash, or salt, or sharp sand around your threatened plants. In theory, snails don't like crawling over such substances. This one has never worked for me. I think the snails learn to jump in the night.

You can go out at night and pick them up by hand, either crushing them or putting them into salt. If you do this every night, you will reduce the numbers. You will also begin to question your own sanity.

Or you can buy commercial snail pellets, and use them sparingly. I confess that when the problem becomes too great for me to simply accept the losses, this is what I do. It's rather sad to see all the empty shells and crippled snails bubbling in their death throes the next day, but it works, and the chemicals involved are not the worst in the world, breaking down quickly.

However, at some stage, before you do any of these things, have a close look at a snail, so you can see the pattern on the shell, and the funny feelers, and the amazing foot. Like most things in the garden, they are really rather appealing.

~

Readers will guess by now that I shop at supermarkets with reluctance. Like most people, I can't avoid them altogether. There are some things — boring things — that are not easily available elsewhere. Once, this was true of toilet paper, but I have since found a company that delivers big boxes of the stuff to your door, with the proceeds going to providing toilets in the third world. 'Changing the world from the bottom up' is their motto, and the name of the company is Who Gives a Crap. We all do, I reply. We all do, like it or not. But I digress.

I have also become a customer of a retailer that delivers to your door, allegedly cutting out the middleman between farm producers and customers. So that looks after bread, milk, juice, and cheese. But as for plastic food wrap, leather-couch cleaner, tinned beans, caster sugar, and flour — if I want these things at reasonable prices then, like almost everyone else, I have to traipse down to one of the big multinational conglomerates that makes its money by bringing produce to the city, becoming the point of interaction between factory, paddock, mine, and home.

I can't remember who it was that pointed out to me that the human body interacts with the outside world mainly through its digestive system. Take the gut altogether, and it has more surface area than our skin. We take the world in through our mouths, and it travels through us, entering our blood streams and making us who we are. The gut also contains more bacteria, I am told, than there are human beings on the planet. We have worlds within us, mostly unconsidered. We are not only ourselves.

So it is with supermarkets and the city. The trucks bring the produce in. From the supermarket, it travels out, in plastic bags, and spray bottles, and tins, and punnets, broken down into modest amounts consumable by individuals and families in the course of a week, finding its way into everyone's fridge, and then into the gut. And then into the rest of our bodies. Then out again, as we give a crap. Ashes to ashes, et cetera et cetera.

These thoughts have been provoked by a trip to Bunnings, which I confess is a favorite place although it, too, is a supermarket, and owned by exactly the same people who are responsible for the loud, antiseptic, brightly lit aisles, and the cheerful songs about discounts, in my local shopping center. Bunnings' garden center, in which you can buy anything to do with the garden, lures me in. I try to collect my own seed. I order online from obscure seed networks and gardening clubs. But several times a season, I end up at Bunnings.

This time, I was after a drip-irrigation system.

To call it an irrigation system seems too grand. After all, it will cover only my tiny space. I need it, though. When life gets busy in summer, my garden tends not to get watered. In theory, I enjoy watering. Standing in the backyard in the evening, hose in hand, my back to the house with all its demands and chaos, can be pleasant. But I don't do it often enough, and with so many things in pots, things die that need not have died with better care.

The components of a drip-irrigation system are not easily available anywhere other than Bunnings (and its competitors). I looked online, and found nothing. Where else will one find these tiny fiddly and arcane things: barbed thirteen-millimeter t-junctions, rigid and flexible four-millimeter riser tubes, punch tools and hole stoppers, variable-flow drippers and fixed-flow drippers, many kinds of each, some on stakes and some on their own. Microjet sprinklers, barbed and threaded end-stoppers, fifteen-millimeter to thirteen-millimeter barbed converters, and more than two dozen different kinds of timed hose-connector, some with mechanical dials that count down the watering time before switching off, and some with computers, and moisture sensors, and WiFi capability, allowing the gardener to water, or not, without leaving the comfort of the living room. It took me almost half an hour to work out which one I needed.

Standing in the checkout queue with my box of bits (including a few plants that were going so cheap I could not resist), I fell to reflecting on what it takes to produce these things. Somewhere in the world, there must be people who have careers in micro-irrigation. There must be people who design those t-junctions and drippers. And off I went, into an imagined world.

The designs, I imagine, are fairly settled. Yet the companies that make these things would, like every other enterprise, be looking for more efficiency. What is the minimum amount of plastic to make a dripper? Can it be lessened? Can it be made more robust, or less robust so people are forced to return and buy more? What is the profit margin on a fifty-cent end stopper? There must be people in offices somewhere whose job it is to figure this out.

And, once the pieces are created, there is marketing. How do they plan to persuade people like me to buy one brand rather than its apparently identical competitor? There must be people with careers in designing the labels, and writing the brochures. There must be brand managers, and departments that liaise with Bunnings to find out how many rigid risers they expect to sell in the month of October. Then there are trucks. Surely they can't fill whole trucks with drippers? So there will be teams of middlemen and women who work out how much can fit, how to minimize the time and fuel spent driving from retail outlet to retail outlet.

Somewhere in the world, there will be people who know things like whether there is a fashion in favor of microjet sprays, or micro drippers. I wonder if they talk about it at dinner parties? What is the conversation at the annual Christmas party? Do they have management retreats? Team-building exercises? Training sessions in which they learn the latest techniques for distributing water to the home garden?

The people who work in this industry must themselves have homes, and children, and pets, and gardens. Whole lives rest on the plastic bits and bobs of home irrigation. The children attend school, and go on excursions. The people go on holiday, and buy toilet paper and plastic food wrap at the supermarket.

I assume, like all of us, they seek the meaningful life, and want to feel part of something bigger than themselves. Some of them will believe in God. Some of them will not. They will be good citizens, and bad. They will volunteer, and get eczema, and suffer from mental illness, and give to charity, and take pleasure in ice-cream. And all of them are connected to me, standing there in Bunnings with my box of plastic bits of irrigation gear.

When I think like this, I wonder why I don't like supermarkets. Really, a supermarket is a thing of wonder. There is beauty in the connections of trade, and in the great complexity of modern capitalism. We live such busy lives. We are so highly specialized. The society that allows me to be a writer allows others to make their way in careers in plastic.

And we are all connected. Supermarkets make the city porous, just as the gut makes our body permeable to the outside world.

As I proffered my credit card to pay the sum of $146.78 cents, benefitting from a special on the tap connector, I was thinking about Walt Whitman.

'I am large. I contain multitudes.' And in the same poem, he wrote, 'Stranger, if you passing meet me and desire to speak to me, why should you not speak to me? And why should I not speak to you?'

And so the water will flow through these tubes, and into my little patch of soil, and I will be ready for summer.

ACKNOWLEDGMENTS

Thanks are due, as always, to my family and friends for their support and inspiration. Some of this material has been previously published in the *Melbourne Review* and the *Adelaide Review*, where I had a gardening column for some time. Before that, I have written about gardening for *Leader* newspapers, *Sunday Life* magazine and *The Weekend Australian*, and elements of the reflections previously featuring in those columns recur here. I thank all the editors and publishers involved for their support and encouragement.